Creative Pathways

Activities that Strengthen the Child's Cognitive Forces

Creative Pathways

Activities that Strengthen the Child's Cognitive Forces

by

Elizabeth Auer, MEd

Waldorf PUBLICATIONS

Printed with support from the Waldorf Curriculum Fund

Published by:
Waldorf Publications at the
Research Institute for Waldorf Education
38 Main Street
Chatham, NY 12037

Title: *Creative Pathways*
       Activities that Strengthen the Child's Cognitive Forces
Author/Illustrator: Elizabeth Auer
Editor: David Mitchell
Copy Editor and Proofreader: Ann Erwin
Layout: Ann Erwin
Cover: David Mitchell
© 2011 by AWSNA, Reprinted 2013, 2015
ISBN # 978-1-936367-22-1

ACKNOWLEDGEMENTS

This book is dedicated to the students and parents of the class of 2011 and the teachers and staff at Pine Hill Waldorf School in Wilton, New Hampshire.

Special thanks go to the following parents, interns, teachers and friends who played an integral part over the years with plays and projects as well as general support.

- Coordinators: Anne Greer, Audrey Fraizer and Joann Maxwell
- Play assistance: Lynda Henry, Paula Iasella, Jim McGinness, Dee Slingerland, Andrew Kennedy, Jim Drapeau, Stu Fraizer, Sue Upton, Karen Guitman, Lorey Johnson, Carmen DiPietrantonio, Beverly Patten, Freya Carter, Andra Grabazs, Baruch Simon, Sara Richardson, Marci Paini
- General projects support: Anne Greer, Gail Coad
- Bell Tower Project: S. Philip and Virginia Brooks

TABLE OF CONTENTS

INTRODUCTION

As a young child I was fortunate to be able to attend a Waldorf/Rudolf Steiner School in The Netherlands. From an early age I was always making things, aided and abetted by the years in the classroom with handwork and woodwork being part of the curriculum. The impulse and the urge to always be making things, to create with my hands has remained with me throughout my teenage and subsequent adult years.

Creative outlets

During the years our children were growing up, I found plenty of outlets for creativity while being a mother at home. House building lent itself to wonderful projects such as building kitchen cabinets, couches, coffee tables, beds and so on. Among other creative delights were illustrating a children's book and a community cookbook, making doll houses, knitting gnomes, making wall hangings. Our little girls became creative alongside, always wanting to do everything themselves and running off with hammers and screwdrivers to do their own thing.

Finding my way to teaching

Through circumstances of life it took me a long time—until I was in my forties—to actually become a teacher of children. Along the way, occasionally I had taught some drawing classes to middle school students and done an occasional stint of substitution for my husband Arthur, a class teacher at the Pine Hill Waldorf School, and when the right time and opportunity presented itself, I found myself in a little queendom of heaven, a small, octagonal-shaped little building aptly named the Manual Arts studio. I had originally contemplated the idea of becoming a handwork teacher, but one look at the studio and that was it!

Ten years of teaching Manual Arts

It was a heavenly ten years. I followed in the footsteps of my predecessors to some extent but added a lot of touches and angles of my own to the curriculum. Sculptural form was my main approach, and not being inclined to be mechanical, I opted for carved tall ships in seventh grade rather than mechanical toys. Being handy with sewing, students sewed the sails in either the handwork classes or in the Studio. Carving in marble in seventh grade was also an added challenge, as was creating a framed stained glass piece in grade eight. In short, the ten years were filled with wonderful projects which the students could be proud of. I learned a great deal about class management and what it meant to instill enthusiasm in students I saw for class once per week.

After-school program

For five of the ten years that I taught in the Studio, I also ran the after-school program each afternoon from 3–5 pm. Children of all ages would come and enjoy the benefits of all the materials and the tools and create endless projects, big and small. Some little children would just sit on the benches and watch others work. Older children could work on their regular projects as well as make something else, do their homework or just socialize. All in all, it was a marvelous time with a fun atmosphere, delicious popcorn breaks and the creation of beautiful objects.

Taking on a class

One of the reasons that I turned towards class teaching after ten years was a desire to use my creativity in a new way, with a group of children I would see every day, and with whom I would also be able to create a more lasting relationship. There would be new projects to take on as the years went along and a new challenge to teach all the eight years of elementary school.

Seeing the benefits

As the years progressed and I observed my students grow and mature, I could see the benefits as we went along. Some were subtle and others were dramatic. Some benefits also remained hidden, lying dormant, sometimes for years. It was always important to keep in mind that results and benefits are not always tangible, and that in many cases what the teacher is able to provide for the students are seeds for the future.

The journey

It would be an understatement to say that this journey has been rewarding. For me there has been no greater joy than to see my students get all excited about the next project, whether it was a play, cutting glass, or creating with beeswax. Ultimately it is all about the enthusiasm the teacher brings to the everyday learning, and seeing that enthusiasm reflected by the children. This was reflected not only in doing projects, but also in drawing, painting and modeling.

Feedback from former students

Recently I ran into two former students who confirmed the importance of working with the hands. One had just come back from Nepal, where he had been apprenticing with a wood carving master. He had returned with some treasures he had carved. I was astounded by his achievements and his obvious enjoyment and pride in his considerable accomplishments.

The other was a young lady who is an expert in restoration of art work. She explained that, because of all the things she had learned to do with her hands in elementary school, she had become so good at being able to tackle all sorts of different aspects of her work.

These are the kinds of validation that bring joy to the teacher—the ultimate reward for providing the opportunities for students to have fun while they are learning and to bring the benefits they have gained into their adult working life and to those with whom they come into contact.

CREATIVITY

Creativity is the heart and soul of this book, which documents a journey through the grades, where each day is a creation unto itself. What is the meaning of creativity and what role does it play in Waldorf education in particular? What are the practical realities of being creative within a classroom setting? How do teachers motivate students to be inventive, resourceful and have creative initiative?

The meaning of the word

To create and to be creative—to bring into being and to cause to exist—generally implies that something new comes about that wasn't there before. The word serves as a verb as well as a noun. Creation itself is applied to the very beginning of the world itself—created out of nothing—world coming into being.

What does it mean to be creative?

Having looked briefly at the definition of the word *creative*, what does it mean for a human being to be creative? Creativity can exist in thinking, the ability to solve problems by looking at things from different angles and coming up with 'creative solutions.' We talk about 'thinking outside the box.' In this context, it seems that creativity provides greater possibilities for finding solutions, rather than the more usual ones. From this we could say that if a child is provided with the opportunity to be creative, her education is deepened.

Creativity in children

Children have an innate need to be creative. From an early age they love to build with blocks, make sand-castles on the beach and draw on paper. They immerse themselves in projects such as cutting things up and gluing them together, making gingerbread houses and making mandalas. At later stages of development they find creative ways of riding their bikes, enjoy making acrobatic flips on skate boards and play music on their guitars. Creativity absorbs the head, heart and hands.

The art of education

Twenty-four centuries ago, Plato made aesthetics the basis of his philosophy of education, where the arts play a critical role in the act of learning. Herbert Read, in his book *Education through Art* puts forward that "the place of art in the educational system is far-reaching. Indeed, the claim is that art, widely conceived, should be the basis of Education. Art serves its purpose as enhancing the learning process. Creativity is embedded in Art."

In his chapter on 'The Purpose of Education,' Read writes that "although it seems obvious that in a democratic society the purpose of education should be to foster individual growth, many problems arise when we begin to consider what methods we should adopt to this end." He believes education should embody all modes of self-expression, literary and poetic, musical and aural—so that the senses are brought into harmonious relationships with the external

world. He summarizes by saying that the general purpose of education is to foster growth of what is individual in each human being, at the same time harmonizing the individuality with the social group to which it belongs.

Waldorf education and the importance of the arts

Rudolf Steiner, an Austrian philosopher in the early twentieth century, founded the first Waldorf School in Stuttgart, Germany. He worked with the first group of teachers to plan the curriculum and how to run the school. His curriculum indications were further developed by subsequent teachers who attended his lectures and meetings. There are many books and lectures on his educational thoughts and ideas. Art was intended to be a central theme, an essential ingredient in the learning process.

The impulse for activity

In *Steiner Education in Theory and Practice*, Gilbert Childs summarized many of Steiner's thoughts on Waldorf education and its practice. Steiner said that it was of great importance to instill from the beginning elementary years the human gift of having two hands that can perform useful work, for themselves and for others. He said that nature is understood with the intellect; only by artistic feeling is nature made

into living experience. The child who is brought up to understanding ripens to ability if such understanding is imbued with life; but the child who is brought up to art will ripen to creative work. In creative work children can grow by their faculties.

The impulse for activity, the urge to do something lies at the basis of human nature, in the adult, as well as the child. Education bridges the gap between the need to be active in play in the child and the need to be active in work in the adult.

The role of art

To be able to practice art the students have to fully immerse themselves in the material. In *Education towards Freedom*, Frans Carlgren puts it this way: "This process of entering into the material often leads to a whole range of feelings in the soul: expectation, disappointment, anger, resignation, thoughtfulness, surprise, new hope, new efforts of will, intense joy at being creative. But it is not only in the soul that this entering into the material is felt. It goes right into the physical body, into fingertips and toes."

The formative powers of art

Carlgren goes on to say that "art is formative, both in the material world and in the world of the soul. Some artistic tasks might require a different inner attitude to the one we instinctively adopt. In this way the cautious child can be persuaded to be more daring, an exuberant child more circumspect, a weak-willed child more persevering, and an obstinate child more adaptable, and so on. As teachers, we can help to make permanent in children another deep-seated instinct: to participate in everything they meet in the outside world, to occupy themselves with it and to try and give it form. There is no other form of activity which is more suitable for cultivating this instinct, even in early childhood, than artistic activity. Through this activity a person learns to enter with all the qualities of his soul and with every fibre of his body into the battle with a problem which is important not because its solution will bring any material gain but simply because it is humanly interesting. Thus the basis is laid in the child for the capacity of taking a real interest in the world around him in later life."

Social benefits

Students working together creatively as a class can be a healing process. Modeling a structure in clay is one example. Another example could be creating scenery for a play, when the class can be divided into groups. The groups are carefully organized by the teacher so that tensions between certain children can have a chance to work themselves out. Each group has a special theme they have to work on, and no one is designated as a leader. They have to work out their design as a whole. Performing a play is the ultimate class artistic activity, in which everyone needs to participate and do their part in order to create a whole experience.

The creative teacher

Creativity in the classroom depends largely on the teacher. Creativity in the teacher comes through enthusiasm for the subject, a love for 'hands-on' learning, and a joy of doing things with children. In my experience of working with children, most boys and girls attain the greatest enjoyment out of doing projects in the classroom. They love to be busy making things. In order for them to be busy making things, the teacher needs to make the time available.

The teacher as provider

In Waldorf schools the days are filled with the students documenting what they learn in their self-made books. The entire collection of books shows the development of the students and what they learn as they make their way up the grades. Page after page shows what they have learned, enriched with artwork to accompany the texts. Aside from the artwork in the books, the teacher can provide the students with opportunities for projects to accompany the study to enrich the experience. What is not shown in the books are the additional projects that the children

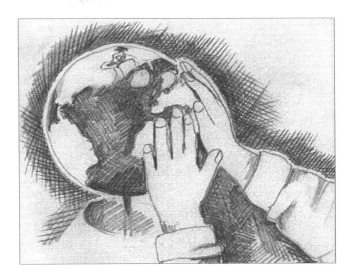

create to further enhance their learning, such as modeling, painting, scenery preparation and the construction of projects.

Creative projects

There is such a variety of projects that one can do with each subject to enhance the learning. Festivals during the year provide wonderful opportunities for creations such as Michaelmas shields and paper lanterns. Modeling Noah's Ark gives the opportunity for third graders to express their love of animals as they model the pairs that go into the ark. Painting a cave scene broadens the experience students can have of mining for crystals and rocks during the Mineralogy block in grade six. The scope is wide and exciting.

Inviting in guests

It is beneficial for students to appreciate other teachers and specialists, especially in the middle school years. A good example of this is to invite an African to teach the class drumming during the block on African Geography in grade seven or eight. Drumming is a specialty that students get excited about but many teachers do not have in their repertoire. Medical professionals can be invited in during a Physiology block.

In the earlier grades spending time with the farmer is a classic example of going out to meet the world, seeing what life is like on a farm—a direct experience for the students. Many students have little idea where milk comes from and how it gets to the breakfast table each morning. Inviting a First Nation storyteller in grade three while the students learn about how the Native Americans built their houses is another example of enhancing the learning. Another example might be to bring in a building specialist for the house building project, such as a post-and-beam builder.

Going out from the classroom to meet specialists or people who can broaden the awareness of students is another avenue. My class went to downtown Wilton in grade four when we were in a block on Local Geography, and the students actually got to shake hands with a descendant from the times when the first families settled in this little New Hampshire town we live in. What a thrill that was!

How can teachers become inspired?

Being creatively inspired is not always a natural gift. Yet I do imagine that if there is a willingness by the teacher to develop creativity, to learn from others, or to take initiative to discover things by oneself, there are ways to catch a spark and let the flame kindle. True, the enthusiasm has to exist in the first place, for without enthusiasm it is hard to become inspired to do anything extra in the daily life of teaching in the classroom. Making prototypes really helps to find and foster the inspiration, especially when what you are making turns out really well!

Inspiration from others

Often teachers are inspired by other teachers and artists. Seeing how others work with children of different ages is important and can be very helpful. Observing in other classrooms is one way of finding this inspiration. One can also learn a lot from reading books and trying things out for oneself. Taking courses is another way of getting the 'creativity bug.' Making marionettes and taking part in a marionette performance was one of the highlights of my experience in taking courses.

Creative geniuses

There are lots of creative people around for the benefit of us all. You have to look around to find them. One of them is Janene Ping, a master kindergarten teacher who specializes in marionette puppetry. I attended one of Janene's workshops and not only made a marionette but also performed in a fairy tale marionette show along with the other participants. This was so inspiring that I just simply had to do it with my sixth grade students, as described in chapter six. Aside from creating my own puppet, working with the other participants was a privilege, as well as deepening my respect for the wisdom of fairy tales.

Funding creativity

A significant number of projects require a minimal amount of funding. However, materials needed for some are fairly expensive, such as using glass for mosaics. Donations can be asked for and scraps can be scrounged, but this is not always possible. Looking ahead as much as possible and being prepared to hunt and search for materials can be helpful.

GRADE ONE

DRAWING

The first day of school

On the first day the children were asked to draw a picture of their summer. As I watched them sitting with their blank paper and new crayons in front of them, I felt the importance of the moment. This was the beginning of their formal schooling and so much anticipation had brought them forward to this first day of school! What a special task the teacher has before her! To guide and to nurture the beings who sit at their desks—to start them on their eight-year journey through the grades.

The first attempts

It was interesting to see that most of the children set to work right away, while some hesitated, too much taken up with the excitement and the newness of the surroundings, as well as the awareness of sitting at a desk and surrounded by other children. Many of the drawings were 'finished' in a very short time, with a lot of empty space on the paper. The illustrations show three examples: one clearly showing 'summer experiences,' the second showing a classic 'house' with a rainbow and two 'figures,' and the third showing a 'family' of four. Other examples were tooth-like mountains and stick figures looking like they were about to dive off a board. Whorls and scribbles as well as smiley faces were other features.

The figures were either stick-like or like a solid post with a head on top, the head being rather large. Skies were for the most part left out with suns appearing in two.

I decided to keep all the drawings made on the first day of each school year and resolved to ask the children to draw a person-house-tree picture three times a year each year through to eighth grade. (As the years went along, the children began to look forward to this special time and eagerly drew their pictures and also gladly gave the drawings up). It was marvelous to have a growing record of their development.

The first formal drawing lessons

Right from the very beginning it was important to establish that everyone's work is good and 'beautiful'—that each child does her best and that the work is admired by the teacher and all children in the class. Perhaps it may seem a little early to be concerned with this, but children are becoming more aware and critical at an increasingly earlier age and stage of development.

For even the young child, a chance remark about his or her drawing by another student can create the beginnings of anxiety that is best avoided. Each child needs to feel free for as long as possible to draw unselfconsciously. Along with creating the atmosphere came the gradual awareness of expectations from the teacher.

Setting the bar high from the start

Children imitate from real life, from example. They naturally follow what the teacher does in the first years. What the teacher shows by example on the board or on paper shines as a living example in front of them. The teacher can set the bar high right from the beginning with clear expectations laid out, appropriate to the stage of development and age of the children. In first grade it may simply go as far as asking the children to take their time and to take good care of their work. Little moments of individual guidance along the way can begin already early on in the year as the teacher gets to know her students. I found that some children were best left alone while others needed help with executing their drawing to their very best ability. It was important not to pass judgment but to offer suggestions and to see what would happen, how guidance would be received.

Blocks and stick crayons

Around the time of taking on a first grade, I became aware about a concern in some remedial resource circles regarding the use of the beeswax blocks by young children. The concern centers around the potential hindrance to the healthy development of the young child's hands when

frequently using blocks for drawing. In addition, encouraging young children to draw with broad strokes may hamper the young child's natural tendency to draw circles, whorls and spirals. The thought is that giving young children pencils or sticks would be more conducive to developing good pencil grips. It would also allow the children to express their innate tendencies to draw archetypal forms with pointed drawing tools.

It was pointed out that the blocks were actually designed for children in the older grades, but came to be widely used over the decades since the 1950s in many, if not most, Waldorf schools.

In my experience the use of blocks provides an opportunity for creating broad surfaces of colors on paper that can be blended as veils of color one over the other. With the writing of letters on a relatively large scale in the main lesson books, the drawings rendered with blocks also provide opportunities to cover large areas with color, rather than small drawings with pencils or sticks done in the slant-line technique to illustrate the writing content.

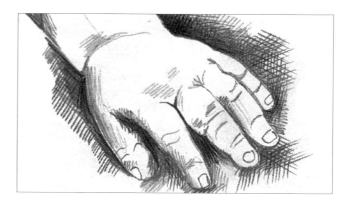

I found that children can be shown and taught by the teacher how to hold the blocks with a grip that does not hinder fine-motor skills in the hand. From my observation over the years, none of my students was delayed in their fine-motor development except for two girls adopted from overseas who had not been afforded the opportunity to move around when they were in their first crucial years of child development. These girls were as able to hold the blocks as any of the other children, but had little coordination in handwork and small fine-detailed activities.

Finger grips

Interestingly, one of the boys in the class came into first grade from another school setting where early learning, including writing, was part of the program. Although (or maybe because he had been requested to hold a pencil at too early an age when his hand was not ready for it) he had learned to write in kindergarten, he had one of the worst finger grips I have ever seen—then or since. He clutched the pencil, stick or block crayon with all his fingers stiffly stretched out downwards. It was almost impossible to relax his grip, and writing for him became a chore. For many years nothing helped, including trying to get him to use a rubber finger grip to allow his fingers to adjust to a more comfortable way of holding the tool. Needless to say, his writing was erratic and caused him stress and challenges all the way through up to grade six. Yet he had excellent fine-motor control when it came to nimble fingers putting together a construction kit, and he became an excellent, regular knitter. Over the years two other children slipped into a less than desirable pencil grip and had to use the rubber grip to remind their fingers.

The use of blocks and stick crayons in the kindergarten

Kindergarten teachers are being encouraged to have stick crayons available in their kindergarten rooms so that young children will more readily be able to draw archetypal forms such as whorls and spirals in a more linear manner. This makes a lot of sense. But the argument does not hold, in my view, for the first grader who is beginning to go on a journey that eventually transforms his drawing ability from linear whirls and spirals to full-bodied drawings showing depth perspective and shadows. While in the kindergarten, young children are given crayons to draw with but are, for the most part, free to draw what they want. Coming into first grade all that changes and the child for the first time receives formal guidance from a teacher.

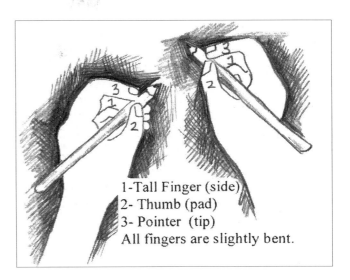

1-Tall Finger (side)
2- Thumb (pad)
3- Pointer (tip)
All fingers are slightly bent.

The ultimate goal

With the beginning of 'drawing instruction' the six/seven-year-old embarks on a journey guided by the teacher towards the ultimate goal of independence in drawing. This journey leads towards gaining an ability to draw linear forms, as well as drawing the world and showing it in its three-dimensionality.

Sculptural form

From the very beginning the student is guided to create shapes with broad surfaces and contours that can be created with the blocks. This is in contrast to making an 'outline' that is to be filled in. The broad surfaces are flat at first, with no roundness and no shadows to create a three-dimensional illusion. (Young children are not yet able to create shadows or differentiated tones of light and dark.) Beeswax sticks in eight or sixteen colors should also be provided for the young first grader to be used for details and smaller areas of shapes, forms and colors.

Time spent drawing

In the main lesson books where children document their work on a daily basis, the drawings bring a deepening to the experience of the subject matter. Drawings are best done after the recall of the story from the day before. This allows the child to work and dwell on her own imagining of the story overnight and up to the point of recall the following morning.

How much to guide

Given that the children have listened to the story and have created their own inner images, the guidance that the teacher offers the students is primarily for those who have challenges with imagination. From the very first day I could see that some children were immediately engrossed in drawing their summer experiences, while others sat there with a far-away look and were barely able to put anything on paper. It is for these children that the teacher can be of enormous help to set them on their path of development in the world of drawing and in the arts in general. The teacher can act as a catalyst for the children's own artistry. In my class there were a couple of children who were at a total loss and needed lots of encouragement.

In the lessons that followed, it also became evident that some of the children were barely able to follow and imitate an example given in front of them, albeit very slowly. Some of these children were also ones who needed to be shown how to hold the block or the stick. I offered basic individual guidance whenever I had a moment, in the hope of inspiring their own inner creativity. For these children it took weeks, months or even a whole year to gain confidence in their skills.

Fostering confidence

One of the ways I tried to make the students feel comfortable and at ease with their own creations was to ask them all to get up from their desks and stand in a circle holding up in front of them the page they had just worked on. This way they could all admire each other's work without looking at their own, or comparing their own work with others.

My first graders experienced a year of joy drawing in their books. I spent a considerable time hovering gently around, taking opportunities to compliment students here and there, and always asking permission to hold up a picture for all to see. They knew that they were safe and could relax without anxiety about whether their drawings were up to 'standard' or not. There seemed to be little concern and self-consciousness. First graders need an environment where they can breathe easily and become engrossed in their creative modes. It is up to the teacher to set the tone from day one, and to my delight and everlasting relief—it worked.

How to guide

I found it a helpful process to prepare a drawing at home for the following day but then draw it again from scratch in front of the children. Bringing in a completed drawing, hanging it up and having the children copy the drawing is not the same as organically 'growing' the drawing with them from the ground on up.

Preparing one's own main lesson book of pictures and text during the summer weeks is ideal but not possible for every teacher. It can be very helpful to lay everything out for the block and to prepare the drawings along with the written material to go in the books. Whenever possible it is best to sketch out ideas for composition and to have at least a good idea of what the basics of the drawing are before drawing in front of the children. In the classroom when it came time to do the drawing, I would recall the images and begin on a white piece of paper the same size as what the students were using.

The guiding process

We would begin with the 'earth' on which we stand and basically set the stage for the action. The 'stage' could be two trees on the outer right and left sides of the paper or a tree and a house, all depending on the action content of the story.

While giving the example on my piece of paper, I would recall the story as we went along, while here and there giving small bits of advice, especially about spatial orientation on the page. Many children have challenges with where to place the elements or have little control at first with managing to fit everything onto one page.

Is the size of objects important?

The relative size of the elements is unimportant—the six/seven-year-old does not yet 'see' the size appropriateness as yet, just as they are blissfully unaware of perspective. I showed how to draw human beings and animals from the head down, while trees and plants 'grew' from the roots up. Everything was kept on a very simple level. All the elements were basically all standing on a flat plane, without any background.

Drawing on the child's level

I found it of extreme importance to do my drawing in front of the children in such a way as to make it possible for them to follow and imitate what I was showing them without straining their abilities. For this reason I rarely heard: "Well, I can't do that!" This meant that I had to really immerse myself into the being of the first grader, to really try to understand what they were capable of drawing in their stage of development.

Leaving some freedom

During the course of the day the children are asked to do many things and to follow what the teacher asks. It seems to make a lot of sense to also allow the children freedom within the boundaries given. Given that we as Waldorf teachers have the nurturing of imagination high on our list of priorities, it stands to reason that if we are guiding the children in their drawing, we also need to allow for individual expression. This can take the form of the children's adding their own details to their pictures, such as squirrels and bird nests, or choosing their own colors for clothes on the figures. I observed how many children loved to add their own embellishments and unique touches, and it gave me much joy to

see with what enthusiasm and enjoyment they would add their own unique effects. They would always ask during this first year, but gradually got used to having certain freedoms and rarely if ever abused them.

The world of colors

The students each received eight colors: lemon yellow, gold, vermillion, carmine, dark green, cobalt blue and violet, both in the blocks and sticks—all together in one pouch. They were shown how to blend the colors and make the colors as rich as possible without creating solid wax-covered surfaces. Light green could be created by bringing the lemon yellow over the dark green, for example, giving in many ways a more beautiful look than what the light green block or stick offers. Having black available on the sidelines was very important and essential, while not readily available in each individual pouch. (Grey and pink were added in grade two.)

The use of black was encouraged to be used for black hair, crows and ants, and anything else deemed appropriate for the use of black. Black is a fascinating part of the color spectrum, being a 'non-color' that embraces all the colors into one whole when they are all combined. It is challenging for the children to create black out of all the colors, but it is fun to show them how it is done. Still, probably the simplest way for them to draw black hair is to just use a black stick.

Black used as an assessment tool

Black can be a useful tool in a remedial assessment when children are asked to draw the 'person-house-tree' picture. According to Audrey McAllen, who pioneered the Extra Lesson work for children with learning challenges, children use the color black in their drawings to express their physical state of incarnation. It is an interesting study in itself to observe which children are attracted to black, how much they are drawn to using black crayons and how much black clothing they wear. In the main lesson books any excessive or seemingly indiscriminate use of black can dominate the entire page. But a little black here and there affords a good balance. Just as with the painting, the children should be encouraged to use colors in all their glory in the beginning years, while shaded drawing with black comes more into its own in the middle school years.

Free drawing

In my first grade there was not a demand for 'free drawing,' as students drew enough pictures in their books to satisfy their needs. Handwork projects were always on the sidelines, readily available—ready to be taken up any time a student was up to date with his work.

HANDWORK IN THE CLASSROOM

The handwork teacher

It was ideal to be the handwork teacher for my own class. (This was made possible because the handwork teacher was willing to take on other duties for the two periods she did not have my class.) The hats that the children were knitting were always eagerly taken up by any student having some spare time before the end of the lesson. There was never a moment of 'boredom.' I always managed, through multitasking, to help any student who needed a dropped stitch retrieved or a color to be changed.

Handwork lessons

As with any other subject, the enthusiasm for handwork emanating from the teacher

goes a long way to instilling enthusiasm in the students. Without exception the whole class loved handwork. There were always opportunities to do special projects during rest time in the afternoon, and it was so handy to have the handwork baskets there at a moment's notice. Having handwork lessons twice a week was a joy, and really an extension of all the other work. For many children this was their favorite lesson of the whole week. Many children learned to knit quickly and well, having already dexterous hands from kindergarten finger-games and finger-knitting. Others were slower and took a lot longer to complete their projects. For the first grade teacher also being the handwork teacher means the extra challenge of keeping all the work in the classroom as well as all the materials handy.

PAINTING

The experience of watercolor

Painting in the early grades is one of the most enjoyable experiences for the class teacher as well as for the students. Children come to look forward to this special time, once a week, and they often asked eagerly: "What are we painting today?" They also felt pride in having their painting up on the bulletin board in the classroom, and especially so if their painting is hanging in the hallway for all to see. The wet shimmering paper and the beautiful colors radiating out towards each other can be a nurturing experience for the young child, where form is not as important as what the colors are 'saying' to each other.

The set-up

Four children were the painting helpers of the month and were asked to stay in for one recess per week to help with the set-up. The set-up included passing out the brushes, the boards, and the water jars half-filled with water. (The teacher took care of the paints and the paper.) The job of painting helper changed each month, so that each child would miss only four recesses per month for half the year. Students at this age can be very adept helpers and actually enjoy doing this task. As with all other tasks, it was important for the children to be helpful and be part of making the painting lesson ready for all their friends and classmates.

Painting trays

After observing many painting lessons in other classes before becoming a class teacher, I tried to figure out how to avoid having to move desks around into squares made up of four desks with a board in between to hold the paint and the water jars. I settled on designing a tray for the side of each desk, running along the edge from front to back (see illustration). This tray held the paint holder as well as the brush and the water jar. Unfortunately because the first grade desk is quite narrow in width, the tray had to be designed according to the desk width. This meant I had to cut off the end of the paint holders to have enough room for the water jar to squeeze in. The paint holders have six round wells to accommodate the six Stockmar paint colors: lemon yellow, gold yellow, vermillion, carmine, ultramarine and Prussian blue. So the design was

excellent while imperfect, but ultimately extremely useful, and not just for the painting lesson. For the rest of the week, pencil pouches, erasers, chalk boxes, and so forth, found their way onto the trays as handy placement for whatever was going on.

The painting lesson

When the children returned from recess, they would settle into their chairs and quiet down while the paper was shared out and sponged, ready for painting. I chose and preferred to do the sponging myself, or have the students do the sponging but then collecting the sponges before beginning the lesson. This avoided the temptation for students to use the sponge to alter what they had on the paper or to mop up puddles.

A hush would settle while the students carefully opened their paint jars according to the colors being used. During these first years usually only one or two colors were opened.

We always began with cleaning our brushes gently and saying a verse, a simple painting verse that set the mood of expectancy. "Now I hold my brush so gently in my hand with loving care. See the colors flow so brightly on the paper clean and clear."

Holding the brush

How the children are shown to hold the brush and apply the paint is of paramount importance towards eventual success with painting. The best way I found to demonstrate the process was by example right in front of them, with paper on a board placed on a music stand, while the teacher stands behind it. This way all the children could have an unobstructed view. I showed them how to move gently and slowly, how to 'pull' the bristles along rather than pushing them upwards and how not to press so hard that the metal of the brush scratched the paper and left nasty marks. Also important was to show them how to dip the brush into the paint, dab off the extra paint on the side of the jar, and bring the brush to the paper without making drips. Getting the children used to the method of cleaning the brush properly by having the 'helping hand' squeeze out the extra water without splashing water drops all over the

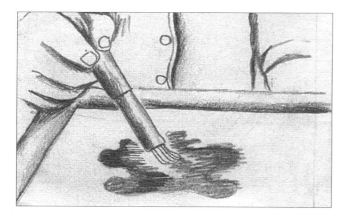

place, including on another child's painting, can be another challenge. The brushes need extra love and care if they are to last over the years.

Guiding the painting lesson

The 'color story' is a truly unique approach to the painting experience for children in the early grades. While it is always a temptation to paint recognizable shapes and forms, letting the colors tell the story and weaving in the connection to the temperaments and soul natures of the colors make for a profound experience for both the class teacher and the children. And while the teacher may guide the painting process in front of the children much like a drawing, the aim here is the experience of the process rather than the eventual outcome.

Painting 'upside down'

For every child to get an unobstructed view, it is handy to be able to stand behind the music stand on which the painting board rests and to

paint from behind while looking down on the painting from above. After some practice this is not an impossible task and is actually quite fun. Certainly with the color stories there is not much in the way of up and down, right or left, so looking at things from a different perspective is not so undoable. (Later on when shapes become more prevalent, painting upside down becomes much more of a challenge, for example, painting animal shapes.)

The paint drips!

When demonstrating in front of the children, having the board at an angle so that they can see provides its own challenge. Paint tends to drip downwards, and this tendency can be greatly annoying especially when forms and shapes are the desired outcome! Yet the children can get used to it, even if the teacher can't and they readily accepted my dripped examples—it did not bother them half as much as it bothered me. Children are our teachers, really.

A reverent atmosphere

The mood of the painting class is even more critical than with any other artistic activity. In order for the students to immerse themselves in the color experience, I found it essential to have peace pervading the room, with no chatting and also no questions asked. I tried to convey from the outset that the painting lesson was a special occasion happening only once per week, and I endeavored to instill reverence for this special activity. Good listening and carefully following my example were what was expected of them.

Different painting styles

As with drawing, individual styles began to become apparent in time. Some students painted very dryly and preferred to have almost no paint on their brush, while others painted with too much paint and made a lot of puddles. Much of this had to do with the control of the paint and the brush, but somehow it also had to do with the children themselves. One very shy boy, who liked everything to be very exact, was always very conservative with his paint, made all his forms very small and when invited to paint freely almost always painted stripes of different colors. Another student always had too much paint and invariably painted her hands as well.

Once a month or so, the children were invited to paint whatever they desired related to the subjects in their lessons, or to paint colors only. This was always a joyous occasion for many and a time of challenge for a few who 'could not come up with any ideas.' After a while they too would take up their brushes and, albeit somewhat hesitantly, begin.

"I'm done. What can I do now?"

Children painting at different speeds and finishing at different times can pose a challenge. It is hard to keep an atmosphere of quiet and reverence if some children who finish get up and begin to clean up and move around the room. A bag of modeling plasticine can be the answer. Children who are finished can put their brushes down, close their paint jars and take out their little bag. Using their hands to quietly model some favorite shapes while others finish up makes it possible to keep the mood to the end, when boards get put away and everything gets cleaned up. The same crew that set up always cleaned up too.

MODELING

The joy of shaping things

Taking a piece of moldable substance into the hands and shaping a recognizable form with it adds yet another aspect to the joy of creating in the classroom. Having a bag of plasticine handy in each desk can provide quick and easy access for any child who has completed an assignment and has some spare time before the next lesson.

The modeling lesson

In first grade the main substance for modeling is beeswax. Beeswax comes in flat sheets of many colors in boxes of fifteen pieces. It is the most lovely, beautiful substance to work with and needs

warmth from the children's hands in order to come to life, as it were, and become pliable. Even when beginning to be worked on, the wax has an enjoyable feeling and becomes a much-loved substance by the children.

Setting the tone

As with drawing and painting, the most important consideration for successful experiences for the child with modeling done in the classroom is setting the 'tone.' During guided times, the atmosphere needs to be on the quiet side and full of reverence for the subject being modeled. When modeling to illustrate a story, the story can be recalled and perhaps become even somewhat of a nature study to help the children keep their focus and also provide time to warm up the beeswax in either the hands or under the armpits.

Modeling can become more of a social activity as is handwork. At times when the students were modeling without guidance, they could 'chat' quietly. There were times when this could be maintained well; at other times some children would get too silly and irreverent, and order and quiet would need to be restored.

The confidence factor

The aim for 'realistic' form by children can begin as early as grade one. The reality is that most first graders are not capable of creating or modeling realistic forms and shapes. Mostly they are blissfully unaware and take pride in what they make. Yet there is a chance that there is already some child, who has an awareness of falling short of the goal of realism. As the children's teacher it became my greatest priority to encourage all the children to be proud and satisfied with what they were able to accomplish. That meant creating an atmosphere of trust and relaxation, in which everything that anyone made was wonderful and to be admired. Whenever there was the slightest insecurity and a child was wondering if her creation was any 'good,' I instantly assured them all that what she was making was beautiful.

Beauty and truth

I recognized from the beginning that there is every grain of truth in telling a first grader that her 'fox' is perfect and beautiful. For in truth it is—it is a 'first grade fox'! This is the representation of the animal that they can manage with their first grade hands, heads and hearts. There is nothing to be 'fixed' or 'adjusted.' I offered as little help as possible and encouraged all the students to do their best. Each one would be happily working on his or her own creation, and we would make a display of them all at the end of the class. Then there was the chance for admiring each other's work—a wonderful community moment for the class.

From the whole to the parts

I showed them slowly and carefully how to bring the head out first from an oblong shape, then form the body and finally 'bring out' the limbs. Many children were able to follow easily, but the two children who had needed help with drawing also needed one-on-one help with modeling. When they were able to 'pull out' the arms and legs, they were short and stubby.

Modeling on the whole became a special event of the week, that, like painting, the children eagerly anticipated. At times, clay was the substance used and lent itself beautifully to creating basic forms such as spheres, eggs, little nests with birds in it, and so forth.

Clay in the younger grades

Children enjoy nothing more than playing in the mud and squeezing it through their fingers, watching it ooze out. Shaping and forming with clay is a wonderful contrast to modeling with

beeswax. While beeswax needs warmth to be able to be shaped, clay is generally cold and moist to the touch and begins to dry out the more it is touched and molded. The students very much enjoyed the time when clay was on the boards for shaping, and they delighted in forming a rabbit shape out of an oblong egg at Easter time.

FORM DRAWING

The straight line and the curve

After beginning the year with a Form Drawing block as an introduction to forming the letters for writing, we continued to take out our slates each morning at the beginning of main lesson to practice forms with our chalks. Basing everything on that first lesson of the straight line and the curve, we practiced circles, spirals, triangles and squares, and steadily the children gained their confidence in working with a moving line. Most children were able to imitate well from examples on the board and to a lively imagination that accompanied the form.

To display or not to display

Occasionally we drew the forms in our books or on paper to hang up on the walls. For the most part, form drawing was an activity to be practiced, rather than an art form to be displayed.

Stick crayons

Children became very adept at using the stick crayons, mostly using the gold first as they lightly drew the forms on the paper. Then when they were satisfied with the form, a darker color was used to go over the form once again. We avoided 'coloring in' the form, but occasionally the outer spaces surrounding the form were given color. I made it a general rule for the children not to use the blocks for any linear drawing, only for creating areas of tones. This way we avoided any cramping of the hand while holding the block.

MAIN LESSON BOOKS

A record of development

The educational journey of each grade is recorded in the main lesson books. This is one of the unique aspects of Waldorf education and affords a most wonderful way to record and observe the children's development over the eight years. It is a source of pride for many as they later look through their books and remember what they studied in the beginning years.

What format to choose?

There are many sizes and shapes of books to choose from. Some teachers choose one main

lesson book for each block. As early as grade one I chose to use the 14" x 17" spiral-bound format, one for language arts and one for math and Form Drawing. Each book had 50 pages.

Language arts

Since the letters come out of the story content in grade one, the drawing would come first after the recall of the story, followed by practice of the large capital letters and eventually the practice of the 'little' letters. I used a format in which the page on the left of the drawing was left blank. The practice of the large capitals and little letters was done on the following spread. Then, later on in the year when we began to write sentences, we revisited the stories and wrote our sentences next to the drawing.

Binding the books together

Using spiral-bound sketch pads or main lesson books eliminates the need to bind the pages together into a cohesive whole. If the books are handled carefully, the spiral binding should be able to last through the year and still hold once the year's work is completed.

However, if time permits, binding the book with covers on front and back and a connecting piece to go over the spiral ridge is a great way to finish them up. (See instructions on pp. 84–86.) They are adapted partially to eliminate the use of rubber cement, which is noxious and, in my opinion, should not be used. Yes! Paste is just as malleable if you have to readjust things—as long as you do the adjusting within a short time limit).

Book covers

For the most part children either painted or drew their book covers. It is nice to start the year off by making simple covers for the books with the children's names on rather than just the plain cover. This initial covering also strengthens the front cover and makes it more durable. However, the students can make another cover for the final binding, as a whole year's worth of shuffling the book around can get it looking ragged on the edges.

GRADE TWO

DRAWING ON THE BOARD

How do you draw a squirrel?

By the second year of school life, the children were becoming very adept at drawing. Whereas in grade one children mostly drew without asking for help, now the children often requested me to draw something on the board that they were doing extra, such as a squirrel running up a tree or sitting on a branch.

Drawing on the blackboard

In grade one I drew mainly on the same size paper as the children used, standing by an easel up at the front of the class. By now the children were used to drawing with the blocks and sticks, choosing their own colors when appropriate, and had learned how to blend colors. This gave me the opportunity to begin to draw on the board. It did not seem confusing to them that they were drawing on a white piece of paper and I was drawing on a black surface.

The board's versatility

The blackboard is a versatile tool for the classroom teacher (as well as the subject teachers). It can be so useful for spontaneous demonstrations as well as for illustrations that remain longer on the board. In grade one I used the board mainly for longer-lasting drawings that were there to enhance the classroom setting, to draw the children into the content of stories, and to give in general a warm atmosphere of beauty, light and color to the room.

Following the seasons

At more or less the beginning of the year I drew two trees on the board, a deciduous tree on one side and a coniferous tree on the other side—all on one of the panels—leaving room for math practice and writing on the remaining part of the board. The trees remained there through the year, changing with the seasons and always having

something new added to them, at least each week if not every day. Gnomes would appear during our math blocks, and elements and characters of our play were added during performance time. Sometimes things magically disappeared to make room for other things. Although the drawing on the board was not for the children to draw in their books, I nevertheless kept it simple, showing no background, no perspective, no shadows, leaving out detail.

The joy of drawing

Drawing on the board is an 'awesome' activity for the teacher—it can be daunting as well as truly delightful. I found it immensely satisfying and fun to draw every picture on the board along with the children, including all the saints and fables we covered in grade two. Sometimes during this year I would just set the stage for the action, leaving them to do the finishing touches and add their own details—beginning them on their path towards independence.

The importance of freedoms

I found it more and more important to give the students freedom wherever I could and felt they could handle it within the boundaries of the expectations. Children do want to express themselves individually and need this outlet to satisfy this need. On the whole those who had this need kept within the boundaries and I did not see inappropriate images appear in their

drawings. This also allowed each student to develop his or her own unique styles.

Recognizing drawings

Over time I came to see and recognize different students' individual styles of drawing and rejoiced in this development, as well as enjoying the mystery of it all. I often mused about how style comes about and how style 'fits' the personality. I made a point of finding a way to praise each child for her effort and special touches, always making sure they were all still okay with my holding up their work and showing it to others. An occasional reminder to the class was given from time to time about the importance of appreciating each other's work at all times.

The first 'drawing tears'

One morning, out of the blue, there was an outburst of tears. "Why, whatever is the matter?" I asked little Geraldine. In between sobs she managed to relate that one of the girls in front of her had turned around and laughed at her drawing. "But surely that doesn't mean that she doesn't like it?" I ventured to suggest. Then in

a calm unperturbed voice, with kindness and clear authority, I quietly but distinctly, once again reiterated to the class that no one was going to laugh at any one's work and that everyone made beautiful drawings. (Neither this incident nor anything like it was repeated during that second grade year.)

THE TEMPERAMENTS

It was fascinating to observe the temperament of each student as I got to know them all and to ascertain how the temperament of each student shone through their drawings and art in general. In a class of 20 students, the four temperaments—melancholic, choleric, sanguine and phlegmatic—are well represented. Generally speaking it was possible to single out the temperaments, though mostly all children tend to be sanguine—and like to run around and jump up and down.

How sad I feel today....

The melancholic temperament manifested itself mostly in the girls. Geraldine in particular was very melancholic. After the crying incident had passed and I had time to reflect on the occasion, I was not surprised at Geraldine's outburst. Her drawings were exquisite and carefully done, and she always took her time over details. She was always fully immersed in her imagination (and was already at this early age able to visualize and place a door at the side of a house.) She, along with Elouise, who was like her in many ways, were intensely shy and quite terrified, for instance, of saying their own lines in a play. Their drawings were quite skillfully executed and always had a lot of details. Interestingly, and maybe surprisingly, the sun almost always shone in their drawings, and bright colors abounded. All the melancholic girls showed sensitivity over their drawings, no matter how sound and good they were, and they were rarely satisfied with what they had done. They also really enjoyed being praised, and I always found every opportunity to let them know how wonderful their work was.

"I can't get the colors dark enough!"

Cholerics tend to do their drawings with gusto and this temperament could be found in both girls and boys. Rushing headlong into the drawing was a general trait, the children preferring not to listen to the instructions and just enjoying doing their own thing. Cholerics tend to not ever need or want help. They loved to be strong with their colors and were for the most part confident that they were on the right track. At times they completed their drawing too quickly and would need some guidance as to how to do some careful finishing. Another aspect of the choleric temperament showed itself in the student's wanting to 'do it over again.'

The question of starting over

I rarely allowed a student to 'redo.' I felt I had to be very careful not to fall into the trap of ripping pages out of books and allowing the student to do things over because he or she was dissatisfied. So a 'do over' was a very rare occasion, and instead of taking pages out, a fresh, new page was glued over the 'offending' page. This was rarely an issue, certainly in the first three grades. (However, if students did sloppy writing that was not up to standard, there were some occasions when the writing would need to be redone, but this did not come much before fifth grade.)

"I'm done. Can I read now?"

This is a question the teacher hears more than any other. Sanguine children have the tendency to flit like butterflies from one thing to the next. Like cholerics, they tend to rush through their drawings, but treat their paper with a much lighter touch. They want to get their drawing done as quickly as possible so that they can get on to the next thing or have some extra time to read. These are the children who can be greatly challenged to slow down and take better care over their work. Most often there is enough interest in the content of the drawing, but the sky gets a scribble and, hey—presto—'it is done'!

Reading as an incentive

Many children love to look at books in the younger years, and once they start reading by second grade, many become voracious readers who always have their nose in a book. Some children fall into the habit of getting their work done quickly so they will have time to get some reading in as well. I caught on to that early on and always found something else for these particular children to do, although encouraging them to take more care sometimes has little effect. Two minutes later the oft-repeated question was asked—"I did what you asked. Now what?"

"But I need more time to finish!"

This is the statement the teacher hears most often from the phlegmatic child who never seems to have enough time to complete the drawings. The phlegmatic tends to plod along slowly, taking lots of care over everything. There was one particular boy who would go over and over the same element—such as the tree—and barely manage to complete just the tree when everyone else was already finished with the entire picture. This poses a true dilemma for the teacher and there are no easy answers.

What to do?

The answers will vary from child to child, but none of the choices is satisfactory. Keeping a child in at recess to complete the pages not only deprives him of fresh air and a break from a stuffy classroom, but also of the ability to move around and have physical exercise. Having him complete the work during extra periods/classes after the main lesson means the other students already finished will get to do other projects or free time activities. Having a student take the main lesson book home to work on gives extra 'homework' and it is uncertain whether the book will come back to school in a timely manner, or for that matter, in one piece or at all. Occasionally a student who was behind would take his book home over the vacation to work on it.

The writing comes first

A general rule began to establish itself as we went through this second year. The written work always had to be completed first—the illustration was like a dessert. I had to establish this because the students were so keen on drawing—many of them preferred to draw rather than to write. (It got worse later on and I had to be quite the watchwoman.)

Writing as an art

As the class teacher I considered the writing to be part of the artistic form of the book and that all students were to strive to write as carefully and beautifully as they could. During the latter half of the second grade year, I introduced cursive writing and we practiced on our slates for months before finally writing our first sentences in our books at the end of the year. This way we prepared our skills to write the Old Testament stories in cursive the following year.

DRAWING ANIMALS

With the fables taking up a considerable part of the language arts blocks during grade two, the children got to practice many shapes and characteristics of animals, birds, fish and reptiles. Several of the saints stories, such as those of Saint Francis and Saint Werburgh, have animals that play significant roles in the stories.

A nature study opportunity

Here is an ideal opportunity for the teacher to bring in a mini nature study lesson, speaking about its characteristics and its habitat before drawing the designated animal. Without exception children love animals and know many things about them already. They usually have a lot to say! So it is a fun way to have a great discussion with the children and allow them to share their knowledge and tell anecdotes.

Simplify the practice

I found it best to always depict the animal from the side view and keep it as simple as possible. Frontal views do not adequately show the shape of the animal and angled views known as three-quarter views do nothing but confuse the young child. Side views show the form in a way that the students can best try to imitate on their own piece of paper. Many children know animal forms intimately and can render them well. Others have a hard time and it's a great challenge to put down on paper the images they have in their minds and memories. The more practice you can give the children the better. To be able to draw adequately what an animal looks like can be felt as an enormous accomplishment. Lack of skills and confidence in this aspect can cause serious consternation to the growing child and can foster a path of shutting down and discouragement, especially as they become more and more self-conscious and reach the nine-year-old stage of development.

PLAYS

Composing a play from scratch is one of the most pleasurable activities and creative opportunities for the class teacher. Each play can be specifically written with the particular constellation of students in mind and include a special role for each child. What play theme appeals or 'speaks' to the class teacher and would be best suited for the particular class is a mystery. It can be an inspiration that appears suddenly, or it can be an idea that grows slowly and perhaps the play is only written at Christmas time. Children love to put on plays and there is a lot of excitement in anticipation of the eventual performance.

The play in the first three grades

The play in the early years usually comes towards the end of the school year and is often short, with mostly chorus and few individual lines, and performed in the confines of the classroom. The classroom is a familiar place to the children and all the rehearsals can take place with the desks pushed to the side. Sometimes several performances are needed to accommodate all those who can fit into the classroom. Plays that are done in the classroom have a lot more flexibility in terms of when they are performed— since there is no need to work with a schedule for a shared space such as an auditorium.

For the most part children are not yet ready to step out and recite more than two or four lines, and all the children learn the whole play over several weeks. Any student can take up any role as they all easily learn all the lines of the play by heart. Lines are mostly rhymed, simple and short and learned orally in increments, adding some more lines one day at a time. Learning the lines can take the place of speech exercises each morning during the warm up exercises. (Individual scripts are typically not given out until the fourth or fifth grade.) Young children have an amazing memory and an ability to learn lines very quickly, much more quickly than the teacher!

How to write a play

It can be a daunting task to write a play, and there are several already written and published plays from which to choose without writing your own. One possibility is to take a play already published and adapt it to your own class and its individuals. The other alternative is to write the play from scratch, to come up with something unique and maybe different or a variation on a theme.

Beginning with the theme

Writing a play may work best going from the whole to the parts, thinking first about the whole concept and then how the parts will all fit together. The experience is a bit like writing a book and putting a table of contents together, the skeleton, before fleshing it out with the actual lines of content. Pedagogical questions, such as what play would be good for the class to experience and would best suit its configuration, are part of the considerations. Perhaps plays you see performed by older classes can inspire you to do something similar but written specifically for younger children. Most often it makes sense to do a play that connects strongly to the curriculum of the particular year.

Writing the lines

Once the theme is decided upon, the type and rhythm of the lines need to be determined. Much can be learned from studying how other plays are written and how they sound. Composing short lines with rhyming words is a lot of fun. Words can be played with and exchanged in the lines just to make the rhymes work, since it is so easy to get 'stuck' on certain lines 'not working.' At times lines that don't work well can be left for a while and returned to later when a fresh look can be helpful and solve the problem.

Additional aspects

It is also fun to compose some music to go with the play, some songs for the children to sing or pieces to play on the recorder. If this is an insurmountable task, it may be possible to collaborate with another teacher willing to help out.

Giving out roles

A lot is at stake for the children and the roles they receive. This is already apparent in the early grades and there is great excitement when the moment comes when the children are told who will take on what role. Some young children are simply too shy to say anything much on their own. At the other extreme are those children who live to act and ham it up in front of others. Keeping the temperaments and the particular needs of each child in mind, roles can be designated that can really help children with their development.

Can the children have input?

From the very beginning early years, I chose to let the children have 'input' as to who they wanted to be in the play. I asked them to write three choices on a piece of paper, and I let them know that I would do my best to give them at least one of their choices. Fortunately—and somehow it seemed miraculously—this worked out for the most part.

Gender roles

In writing my plays, I found it important to consider roles for the girls, especially in the male-dominated Old Testament stories. To make roles to fit the students in the class is an enjoyable challenge. Sometimes characters in the play have to be added or invented, just to make it work. It was fun to switch some of the genders in short,

humorous skits with some of the boys dressing up as girls.

Helping with scenery and props

It is fun for the children already at this age to help with scenery and prop-making wherever they can. Some students relish becoming props caretakers during the play if certain things have to be moved or set up. I preferred to keep things very simple and have minimal scene, prop and costume changes. Some parents like to help with costumes and the play itself.

Performances

It is wonderful to perform the plays for the whole school. This means that if the plays in the younger years are done in the classroom, depending of course on the size of the room, the 'school' has to come in parts! Perhaps three grades at a time might fit in the audience space, and parents and friends often want to attend too. In this case the class can be prepared to give at least three performances. This is quite an undertaking for the teacher but every bit worth the effort to see the joy that the children experience in performing for their friends, families and other students.

Enriching the curriculum

Plays are a wonderful tool for deepening what is learned in the classroom. What seems to be most suitable or fitting for the class can sometimes become apparent only as the year goes along.

FESTIVALS

The celebration of festivals marks the seasons and different times of the year and play a big part in many Waldorf schools. Festivals afford great opportunities for creative work such as decorating Michaelmas shields and carving pumpkins. There are two big events in this second grade year, namely St. Martinmas and Santa Lucia. Both these stories lend themselves to beautiful celebrations, having to do with the light shining in the darkness in November and the turning of time in December with the coming of the winter solstice. St. Martinmas celebrates the life of the Roman soldier Martin, who, as legend has it, shared his cloak with a poor beggar. The festival is celebrated on November 11, when darkness descends by 5 pm and children and families sing songs, light their lanterns and walk along the forest paths.

What kind of lanterns?

There are different ways of creating lanterns. Holes can be punched in patterns in a thin metal material such as sheets of copper fashioned into a simple tubular shape. Balloons can be blown up and decorated with tissue paper on the outside. When the glue is dry, the balloon is popped and the tissue shell holds the shape. Another way the lanterns can be made is with painting paper formed into a tubular shape with windows cut out and tissue paper glued from behind. Or, the painted paper can have slits cut into the middle allowing the light of the candle to shine through the middle and giving the lantern a more Chinese lantern look.

For Michaelmas, my class enjoyed making their own individual shields (as well as decorating the larger class shield) and carried them proudly in the procession. They made drawings of dragons and glued them on to their shields.

GRADE THREE

The nine-year-old change

Grade three is a turning point where the children go through a change familiarly known as the nine-year-old change or 'crossing the Rubicon.' Children begin to separate themselves from the world and become more individual beings. One of the most beautiful ways to begin the year is with the great and momentous stories from the Old Testament, especially the stories written by Jacob Streit in *And There Was Light!* This small booklet is a gold mine of treasures. Streit is a master storyteller and brings the seven days of creation in a most moving and beautiful way for the nine-year-old. Certainly in my experience, the stories afforded a most memorable week of recreating and orchestrating a one-of-a-kind main lesson.

PAINTING THE CREATION

Each morning for the first six days of school, after saying the verse and recalling the story from the day before, the children began the day with painting. Everything was prepared the day before and all that remained to be done was sharing out the paper. Then the painting began with children immersing themselves in the colors and the wet paint flowing onto the paper, yellow meeting blue as a first painting. To my mind, in all the eight years of elementary schooling, this came closest to a religious experience for both the students and the teacher. The freshness of the new day, the profundity of Streit's stories, and images make for an outstanding moment of teaching in the classroom.

And there was light!

The very first painting took us back to meeting blue and yellow in grade one, recapitulating on a more sophisticated scale this amazing combination: the lemon yellow streaming downwards and being cradled in the passive, beautiful blue below. There is no form or shape to see, only the experience of color.

Children can be shown how to soften the edges of the blue by beginning down below and slowly moving upwards to meet the light, but never quite touching the yellow.

The separation of air and water: the condensation of matter

There are two possible ways to have the children experience this second day of creation. One way is to work again with blue, and bring about a lightness in the blue above, so separating the waters from the air. For the second day, Streit brings in images of air-angels fanning the glowing earth-fire and light-angels pushing down all that was heavy, thus creating an above and a below. I chose to go with the contrasting warm colors to create the image of the condensation of matter. We began with lemon yellow at the top and slowly worked our way with gold, followed by vermillion, to finally end with the carmine below, perhaps giving a feeling of flickering flames, but no forms as such.

The formation of land and the first plants

In this painting of the third day Streit brings a most beautiful story of the cooling of the earth: the cool waters rushing to the depths, the fiery light to the heights, the solid ground forming on the sea floor. He relates how the lily plant begins to grow and develop, bringing its stems from deep down below in the depth of the waters up to the

light. This lends itself to a most beautiful and enjoyable painting experience. Beginning with the top half in lemon yellow and the lower half as the blue water, the land appears down below with a little vermillion on the brush. Then with lemon yellow, the plant stems are brought up from the depths and come up to the surface and spread themselves out into lily pads—a beautiful green with the yellow mixing into the blue. Finally, to complete the painting, the lilies appear in the bright sunlight, either as white shapes created with the dry brush into the yellow or as golden lilies painted into the lemon yellow.

The sun, moon and the stars

This painting is another treat—there is no other way to express the enjoyment of it. Lemon yellow and blue again divide the page in half—this time vertically. While the lemon yellow is left to dry a little, the shape of the moon and a small circle for each star are created with a dry brush until the space is as white as possible, with the moon's sickle bending towards to sun. Lastly the golden sun is painted right over the yellow, and lemon yellow makes the moon shine and the stars sparkle. (You can, of course, paint the sun in right away before the moon and stars, which makes more sense since the light of the sun is reflected by the moon and the stars.)

The birds of the air and the fish in the water

Once again we began with the lemon yellow above and the blue below, creating air and sunshine and deep ultramarine ocean water. The shapes for the fishes can be created by a dry brush or painted into the blue with the Prussian, while the birds of the air can be painted in with gold and a little vermillion.

Animals and the human being

This last painting is the culmination of the series and can take the form of a simple human shape, gold on yellow, or a human form in a landscape with a tree on one side and an animal on the other. The simplified human form could also have an animal shape down below at its feet. I chose to place the human and animal forms into a simple landscape created out of painting all the colors first, moving from lemon yellow to gold, to vermillion, to carmine, and finally to blue, blending some blue into the carmine creating violet and green. With a little vermillion, a tree was created. Then with a dry brush or gold, the human being was added, followed by perhaps a deer with a little vermillion.

Color on the walls

With their beautiful bright colors and variety of subject and form, these paintings made a beautiful display on the bulletin boards and accompanied the whole Old Testament block for the month of September. Subsequent paintings during the year were a wonderful experience, too, as Noah's Ark appeared on stormy seas and Moses went up the mountain to find Jehovah speaking from the burning bush.

MODELING

Noah's Ark

This wonderful children's favorite lends itself beautifully to modeling with beeswax as well as with clay and can afford weeks of enjoyment. Before modeling the animals each student created their own Ark out of clay on a little plywood board 10" x 10". The following modeling class they were happily busy with pairs of animals, modeling with the greatest enthusiasm and focus. Their own little Noah family with animals grew as the weeks went by until the little boards were bursting with treasures. When the modeling time came to an end, they all got to take their work home, after admiring each other's work in the classroom.

Modeling themselves

One of the most fun things to do with the children is to have them model self-portraits. This activity turned out to be one of their favorites. This activity is probably only possible if there is very little self-consciousness and the students are comfortable modeling something so personal as their own being.

FARMING AND HOUSEBUILDING

The third grade is a very busy, 'practical' year. It is filled with activities, large and small, in both the fall and the spring, in and out of the classroom. Every elementary school year is special in its own way and this year in particular takes the children out of the classroom perhaps more than any other year.

The fall

The fall is a good time to do a 'house-building' project. The children have learned about the Native American ways of building houses as well as modern house-building with either the old post-and-beam method or the more ubiquitous 'stick' method of using 2 x 4s. Going out and seeing a modern house being built in its early stages is a wonderful field trip activity.

Deciding what project to do will need careful consideration and depend on the 'culture' in the school and the available parent help and funds. Projects can take a great variety of shapes depending on many factors and the particular environment of the school.

Is there any room left?

At our school, many projects had been done over the years and the property was dotted with different little play-houses, sheds and even a little greenhouse. Different classes had built a patio with bricks under the south balcony, a Sukkoth in the woods, a wooden bridge, and a stone playhouse. What could we do?

The bell tower

Our class chose to do a bell tower to replace an old post and provide a new home for the old bell. Since measurement is one of the subjects studied in grade three, making a structure out of wood gave us a great opportunity to take out the tape measure. With the help of a post-and-beam wizard (parent alum who has a local post-and-beam business), we discussed the possibilities at length, drew pictures and designed it together. We began digging the foundation hole in September.

With the help of parents, we were able to pour the cement down the foundation tubes by November—just before it got too cold. The hole was filled and all was 'put to sleep' for the winter. Come spring and the snow melted, we went to the workshop to see how the beams and braces were created. With great excitement the day came when the posts and beams arrived, went up in the air and were joined up together.

The roof and the shingle factory

Because the tower was beyond our reach, the roof structure was made as a separate unit and kept on the ground to be shingled. Meanwhile we were all very busy at work making the shingles out of pine stumps. The pine needed splitting into half-inch thick shingles that we then nailed onto the horizontal planks of each roof side. This proved to be no mean task and it took a LOT of shingles to cover the whole roof. We measured one side of the roof and laid out the shingles on the ground; then we knew how many shingles we needed for the other side!

The ice-cream on the cake

Finally the exciting day came when our parent builder came with his crane truck and hoisted the roof up on top of the beams. To our great relief it fitted perfectly and was joined to the post-and-beam structure to complete the building project.

The new bell!

The only thing remaining to be done was the hanging of the new bell. It was big and beautiful and had been painted a deep blue. It wasn't long before we had a bell blessing with the whole school and all the children got a chance to make it ring. Later we created flower beds on either side of the tower, with large stumps as seats all in a circle around it. Many a time we sat on the seats and enjoyed a snack or lunch in good weather. Each year following we kept up with the little flowerbeds each spring and planted impatiens in the shade of the trees.

The garden

Gardening is part of the farming block in grade three, and beside the designated third grade flower and vegetable beds, we grew large gourds

to harvest and decorate. We weighed them in the classroom after harvesting and again later on to see how much weight they had lost to 'drying out.' Where had all the former weight gone? We grew vegetables and flowers all mixed in with each other and harvested the marigold petals in October to give to the kindergarten children to use for dyeing silk.

Morning glories

Growing a giant sunflower is a wonderful support for morning glories! Originally the support had been the bean tepee, but somehow a sunflower grew up among the beans and shot so high into the sky, even the morning glories never reached its height. We also created a scarecrow by tying thick tree saplings together and dressing it in

old jeans and a shirt. (We stuffed those garments with straw and it was fun while it lasted.)

CRAFTS

Carding, spinning, weaving and dyeing are the main crafts worked with in this third grade year. Mat weaving with reeds and carving totem poles are also possibilities, as are making coil pots with clay. These are the most wonderful crafts and connect especially to the Native American legends and the First Nation peoples who still live in this amazing land and are also part of the third grade study.

Weaving

The Navajos in the hot dry lands of Arizona and New Mexico make the most beautiful weavings, and we chose to weave Navajo-style on our own individual looms. The Navajos have their

loom structure tied to tree branches as they sit in the shade on a blanket with their own handspun yarn and shuttles. Young Navajo children help to card and spin the wool into yarn. They are built small looms out of wood and taught to weave by their grandmothers.

Preparing the looms

Already in the spring of grade two we had prepared our looms. I cut out the pieces and each child took a turn at helping to put her loom together. (See instructions on pp. 89–91.) This was a wonderful process that included sanding, drilling holes and putting in screws. Once the basic loom was constructed I prepared the warps for each loom. This is a tricky process and is best done by two adults.

The colors and designs

Studying the Navajo colors, I chose to get mostly earth-tone colors that included browns, grays, reds and pinks and black, and yarn that had a real woolly, slightly rough, texture. We looked at the designs in books and each child was free to design his or her own piece—as they went along. This gave them a lot of freedom making their

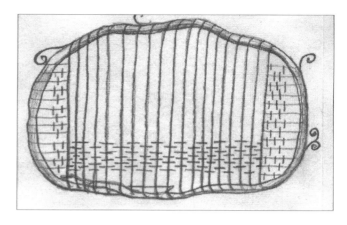

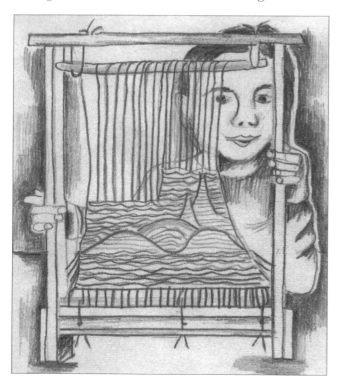

weaving designs within the confines of simple weaving process of back and forth on a warp. They could build triangles, squares, rectangles or simple stripes, arch colors for a rainbow effect, or even create a simple landscape.

Completing the weaving

The maple sticks were left on the weaving and tied in by the ends of the warp. This framework provided a suitable and natural way of hanging the weaving. To tidy up all the loose ends, a piece of backing felt can be sewn on the back and all the loose ends are tucked in.

Alternative looms

Weaving on a loom made out of grapevine boughs is also a wonderful craft. The looms are much less complicated to construct. Grapevines are abundant in New Hampshire and can be found in various places in the woods and at the roadside. In other environments perhaps other vines will serve for this purpose as long as the vines are supple and bendable to suit the loom construction.

Shaping the loom

The loom can vary in size, depending on the time available for the project. (They can be hung on the classroom wall while the project is in progress and in the end make wonderful wall hangings to take home. The weaving process is the same, and can get complex with forms interlocking or even showing a landscape. Students can be given the freedom to use their own choices of colors and shapes.

Dream catchers

While absorbing the studies of the Native American peoples and how they lived and built their houses, making a dream catcher was a highlight of the year. For this project the grapevine is also an excellent source of material. Not only can the children harvest them themselves, but they look natural and beautiful. It also simplifies the process by eliminating the need to wrap an alternative circular form.

Grapevine as frame

Harvest the grapevine and use it soon after while it is still supple. Bend and shape the grapevine into a circle and tie the vine together where needed to keep it in the desired shape. Try to keep the curly pieces of the vine wherever possible—they add so much to the overall look once the project is completed.

Different methods

Try two different methods of making the web first and decide which one would work best for your students. First try the method that you will find in conventional instructions for dream catchers, using only one thread for the whole web. Beginning with tying the thread to the top, bring the thread over to the right approximately two inches, tie it around the frame twice and repeat the action, going all the way around the frame. Make a second round, this time tying the thread into the middle of the first two-inch stretch of thread, knotting again twice, pulling the thread down tight. The first web shape should now look like a diamond shape. Go all the way around and continue knotting until a small circle hole is left in the middle, all the while pulling tight and holding the tension. Finish up the thread with a tight, secure knot in the middle.

The second method is more laborious, but perhaps easier for the students as less tension/pulling is involved. Tie same-length (approx.) 12" threads from the frame at 2" intervals all around. Beginning at the top, tie two threads together into a triangle shape and repeat this action all the way around the frame so all the threads are tied. Begin another round, and tie the threads together all around, this time creating diamond shapes. Keep knotting until there is an empty space left in the middle as with the first method. Cut the leftover threads to ¾" and glue them lying down in one direction around the shape of the hole. The students will need help with this.

Decorating

Once the web is completed, the children can decorate their catcher with beads strung on a string and feathers dangling from the bottom or woven through the web. Alternatively, students can decorate as they go along with the knots, but this is more complicated and can be challenging.

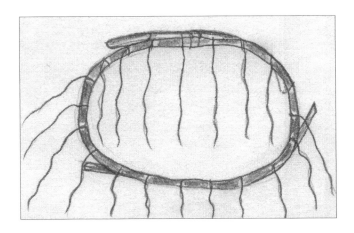

GRADE FOUR

This year brings a new stage with the children, having gone through the 'nine-year-old change.' They are ready for new challenges, not only in the arts but also in language skills and math. Studies of such subjects as fractions, parts of speech and local geography speak to this stage of beginning to look out more wakefully into the world and to grasp its meaning.

A transition time in drawing

Having worked with the beeswax blocks and sticks up to this point, the students are ready to begin a transition to the use of colored pencils for drawing. The size of the main lesson book can be reduced, thereby affording a smaller area to cover on each page.

Leading to the ultimate goal

The goal is for the children to be able to create beautiful surfaces and textures with their drawing utensils, to be able to draw images in sculpturally shaded form with breathing tones and edges. Transitioning from blocks and sticks to pencils is a big step. The pointed pencil takes more time and effort to cover the same area that was covered by the blocks, and it is challenging for the fourth grader to get used to the sharp point of a colored pencil and create smooth texture on the page at first. Children generally tend to do the details carefully and then want to fill in the background quickly. This tendency leads to large scratches of color, diminishing the quality of the overall picture.

Introducing the slant-line technique

Creating short diagonal lines, one closely next to the other, creates a rich, aesthetic texture and tone. This technique allows the student to move the hand rhythmically back and forth, with the stroke going from the top right to bottom left. Whether to lift the hand up after each stroke or to let the utensil hover back and forth on the paper is a question of technique. It takes a lot

more effort for the student to lift the hand after each stroke. To simplify the transition it may be best to wait with the more exacting lift-off stroke until the middle school years.

The beeswax stick crayon versus the pencil

Drawing with beeswax sticks can be a good first step along with the introduction to the slant-line technique. The stick has a blunter point than a sharp-pointed pencil and covers more area in the same amount of time. Children can blend the colors the same way as with the blocks by drawing one color over the other or having colors 'lean in' on each other.

Mastering the technique

Many of my students took to this new technique with relish and created very beautiful drawings. For some the discipline was very challenging and the tendency to want to direct the utensil in any direction was quite strong. I felt it was important to observe just how each individual adjusted to the technique in his or her own way.

Allowing for differences

One student was quite unable to do the stroke in the diagonal, top right to left bottom direction. She was receptive to the technique but had to direct the strokes up and down vertically. Her drawings were very distinct and had their own unique look to them. One student in particular

took to the technique like a duck to water. She formed a 'style' all her own and became the great slant-line technique artist of the class, the other students much admiring her work. What was surprising about this was that she had come to the class as a strong 'outliner' in third grade, all the signs indicating that she might be hard to bring round to a more sculptural way of drawing.

Seeing perspective

This same student also possessed a rich imagination, including an early ability to perceive perspective. The first signs of this new, awakening ability to perceive usually come with the drawing of a house, showing a three-quarter view with two sides. Up until this point houses are generally always drawn straight on, showing just the front of the house. This new ability begins anywhere from grade three to grade five. With some children it takes until later in the middle school to 'see in perspective.'

Teaching perspective

Perspective is taught as a block in the seventh grade. In the years leading up to grade seven, perspective can come gradually into the teacher's drawings on the board, one step at a time. This can begin with small steps in the fourth grade and accelerate from grade five on up. The reality is that many, if not most, of the students will be greatly challenged to draw in perspective much before grade seven. So drawing in perspective on the board can be challenging for students to

follow if they are using the board drawing as an example for their own drawing.

DIORAMAS

Children enjoy nothing more than studying animals. Along with the study of animals comes an opportunity to assign the children an individual diorama project with the animal of their choice.

Different choices

There are several ways to go about this, each one having its own merit. One way is to give the assignment as a project to do at home and then the children bring them in to school. They are free to choose the size and shape of their animal's home and the materials they use for both the environment and the animal. The written work is also done at home within stated parameters.

THE NORTHERN FLYING SQUIRREL

The Natural History Museum in New York

Having visited the museum and admired the amazing dioramas, I had an imagination of a 'museum' of dioramas in the classroom, all with the same format but all distinctly unique. I made up a four-sided box template out of cardboard, cut out 18 of them and then constructed them—ready for the students to take home and work in them. I could get two dioramas out of one three-panel display board. I used duct tape to secure the edges together. (See instructions on p. 93.) Water as part of the display inside could be simulated with blue crepe paper. The basic materials used had to

be natural, such as grass, plants, moss, rocks and stones, sand and shells, and the animals were to be made out of beeswax or clay.

The last touches

When the students brought their dioramas back to school, we pasted on the background drawings that had been prepared in class and decorated the outer cardboard sides with painted watercolor paper.

Exhibition time

The day before the exhibition we had a session for freshening up any wilted branches or dried up moss. All the dioramas were in the classroom and there was quite some excitement. We went outside to collect a variety of nature's gifts—branches with red berries, spruce, hemlock and pine branches, nuts and seed pods, mosses of all kinds—and laid them out on a central table for all to use.

A flurry of activity

Bringing nature's beauty into the classroom brought on an excitement such as I had never witnessed. Greens were freshened up, things were added, things were changed out— 'spruced up' is really the right expression. Some children changed the whole look of their diorama completely, and mostly enhanced what they had done before. They inspired each other as they worked side by side.

The museum look

At exhibition time the students were proud to display their works of art, along with their written work, and some of them gave oral presentations. The collection displayed all together made for a marvelous show and turned into a real fourth grade animal study museum.

MODELING

The Norse myths provide a wonderful opportunity for making a colorful hands-on project of multiple worlds. I provided the students with a construction of wood that had three levels. The base was for the realm of Nifelheim. The middle 'floor,' Midgard, was for humans. The top floor was for Asgard—the home of the gods. A tree grew in the middle, with long roots coming down under it into Nifelheim. There the dragon was lying, chewing at the roots. There were so many characters to be modeled: towers and buildings, a rainbow bridge, a dragon, and even the long snake surrounding Midgard. We spent quite a few modeling classes working on this project, and with each additional figure or animal, the very rich and colorful display grew.

A delightful variety

The children worked in groups and often collaborated on a particular god and his goddess, a cart with goats, or a steed with eight legs. The array of the diverse characters, animals and creatures of all sorts and shapes lent itself ideally to the modeling experience. Students gravitated to modeling characters that had spoken to them strongly as they listened to the myths unfold in the sagas of the Norse Gods.

Odin the Wanderer

For our play 'Odin the Wanderer' we created shields for the gods. Even though there were only a half dozen gods that used their shields in the play, all the children made their own.

The shields were cut out of plywood in an oval-rounded shape and spray-painted silver. We began by drawing linear forms that had to interweave, typical of the Norse forms. The students spent some time practicing their forms

and each form was uniquely their own. This was followed by choosing colors of wool yarn and braiding a long rope, knotted at each end. The rope was laid out on the shield in its interweaving form and then glued on to the shield. Two holes were drilled to accommodate a handle.

The Futhark

The alphabet of runes named the Futhark can be imprinted on clay tablets as well as written in the main lesson books, one letter at a time. This fascinating alphabet was used by the Norsemen in ancient times and is known as one of the first alphabets used. To document legends of old, angular marks were scratched into stone and survive to this day.

I drew the letters in large size on individual sheets and taped them up above the blackboard, much like what I had done with the regular alphabet in the first three grades. Each rune had the name of the letter underneath. In the main lesson books, each rune also had the regular alphabet equivalent written underneath. The students enjoyed writing their own names with the runic letters and had them as name tags on their desks.

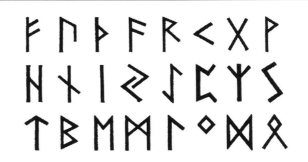

GRADE FIVE

This year is often referred to by Waldorf teachers as the 'golden year.' What that means is that the children have one foot in the energized stage of pre-pubescence and the other foot is lingering on in the realm of a dreamier childhood. Bodies are still lithe and supple, and it is a great year for the Greek Olympic games. The Waldorf curriculum, in my opinion, is never more appropriate for the age group and the child's development than it is in grade five. The main overall theme is looking back to Ancient History and the cultures of India, Persia (Iran), Mesopotamia (Iraq) and Egypt, leading on to the time of the Greeks.

CLAY MODELING

Clay modeling comes into its own in grade five, and what better way to begin than to model the Buddha. A pensive and reverent mood accompanying the activity, little Buddha figures approx. 6" in height began to appear, most of them sitting figures with crossed legs. Some of the children were able to make details such as the hair on top of the head and praying hands. The elephant, a classic Indian animal and beloved by all the children, followed the Buddha. Modeling animals standing upright with clay gives challenges that can be overcome in the following way. We began with a rectangular shape about 5" x 7" x 3" with a somewhat slightly larger base area. We first brought out the head and the trunk,

followed by rounding off the trunk of the body over the top. Then came the process of 'bringing out' the four legs, leaving the underside of the body solid. The legs had more of a relief look rather than a fully rounded three-dimensional form. With this approach all the children were able to be successful in creating their form. There was no worry about the legs collapsing under the weight of the large body. The students were equally taken with this experience, as the study of animals is a guaranteed enjoyment.

Mesopotamia

The ancient story of Gilgamesh lent itself well to creating two figures wrestling with each other. Wrestling was also an activity the students were learning during their movement classes. We began

with a solid lump of clay, about 6" square. Mindful to leave a base for the figures to be grounded on, the students had a choice of either making two figures separately and then arranging them together in a wrestling pose or they could bring both the figures out of the clay from one lump and form them both together. The first option of separate figures was the preferred choice for those who felt more challenged by this assignment. There is a tendency with some children to always want to make the figures too small—and then it is too challenging to add in any details.

GEOGRAPHY

The study of North America afforded the wonderful opportunity to model the map with the surrounding oceans as a whole class. We modeled ours in clay, and groups of four took turns working on it, bringing up the mountain ranges and demarcating the rivers and lakes.

The map and oceans measured approximately 3x3 feet square. The oceans were given a rippled look. Once the clay was dry enough, it was fun to paint the map with condensed watercolor paint and then add three-dimensional effects. Each child took on modeling in colorful beeswax some animal, plant or fish appropriate to certain particular states. Whales, dolphins and seals appeared in the oceans, as well as a tall ship.

Individual states

Once this was accomplished the students created their own smaller maps of the individual states they were studying. The board they worked on measured 12" x 18", and this time they all used playdough, prepared at home and brought into the classroom the following day. Playdough lends itself well, if not better, to map-making. It works well for bringing up the mountain ranges and takes the paint well. It also does not come off the board as clay can tend to do once it is has dried.

The states museum collection

Students modeled the state bird, flower and tree out of beeswax and decorated a display board to accompany the modeling as well as a written report. The display boards were all of uniform size, and the name of the state was written in large letters 2" high. The remainder of the decoration of the board was up to the individual student. Placed together at the final geography exhibition, the collection looked once again like a mini 'museum.'

DRAWING

During this fifth grade year the students finally received their own pencils. The slant-line technique turned into what is often termed as 'shading.' Shading is really another term for 'coloring.' Moving the pencil back and forth over the surface of the paper with small back and forth strokes can create a smooth texture much like that created by the blocks. With shading, the strokes can move in any direction, not only from top right to bottom left.

Drawing the leaf

During the second Botany block in the latter half of the year, we studied the leaf. Students practiced their shading in a way that really brought out the full beauty of this approach to creating smooth and breathing surface tones.

We first drew the leaf 'organically.' From the stem outwards and upwards to the outer curve of

THE PLAY

'Ancient times long ago'

It is important at this stage of the children's development to provide an opportunity for them to create their own scenery designs for the play, whatever the play might be. In our play "Ancient Times, Long Ago," all four cultures of India, Persia, Mesopotamia and Egypt were represented in tableaus. The class was split into four groups, each in charge of the set decoration for their section of ancient history. Each group had a panel 3' wide by 8' high to decorate. The only thing they had in common was a basic circle motif, cut out of golden board, as a basis for a sun-worship design. With some guidelines from the teacher for the appropriate symbols that went with each culture, the members of each group consulted with each other and came up with their own 'set.' Each student also had a hand in creating his own headdress. They were cut mostly out of poster board and stapled at the back. Some students had masks that were provided and then covered with poster board and painted appropriate colors.

the leaf leading to the point. Then, keeping the central mid-vein in mind at all times, we began to bring darker tones to the areas between the veins, making the veins 'stand out.' This approach created the veins by leaving what is known as 'negative space' and is the opposite to drawing the leaf as an outline with veins drawn in the 'positive.' Once the leaf was there in its fullness, a background was given, begun with dark tones on the edges of the leaf and fading out to light. The background completed the drawing study.

Borders or no borders?

With the smaller size of the main lesson book, a smaller format illustrating with a pencil is manageable time-wise for the most part. The question of whether to have the children create borders on each page can be answered in different ways. Borders look great and can enhance the written work in the books. However, I found that borders take up too much precious time of the main lesson's two hours. I devised to create each page of writing with the illustration underneath. This meant that sometimes the images under the writing would overlap into the writing, creating a lovely effect. In the case of overlaps, the color needed to be light and gently applied so as not to obscure the writing. (I always had this rule: Writing first—then drawing.)

The drawing ethic

At this stage of the journey, every student was happy to be drawing, most of them content with their ability and their skills. According to their temperament, some were still in a rush to complete and go on to the next thing. The temperament in some children can at times get in the way of progress. Consistent advice to slow down and take more care does not always have its desired effect. By and large the students continued to be respectful of each other's work, admiring that of others from time to time. This ethic allowed all the children to feel good about what they could accomplish. Occasionally there would be some offhand comment, mostly connected to painting.

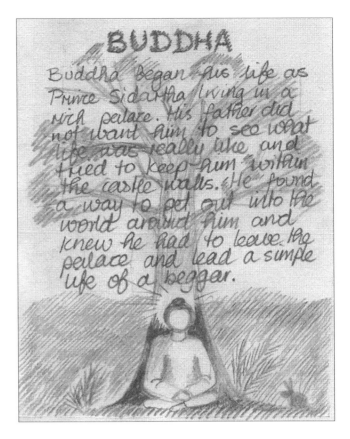

PAINTING

The elephant is a marvelous subject for painting—especially with an African sunset in the background. There is also the classic pyramid scene from Egypt, with the blue sky and hot yellow sand, the Nile in the foreground and palms along the river edges. The Greek temple is also a great subject—a dramatic sky above a golden temple with pillars, and a rocky foreground with cypress trees and boulders.

We also painted the map of the United States, on dry paper taped onto the board. Land areas were painted first, followed by the oceans. First a layer of fairly thin paint was applied over the whole ocean area, leaving a very small 1/8" gap of white between the land masses and the ocean. After this layer of paint was dry, another layer of paint was applied, beginning about an inch away from the land mass. More layers of paint followed, slowly making the ocean darker (and deeper) towards the periphery of the paper until finally the outer edge was reached.

Veiling

I introduced my class to veil painting towards the second half of the year. (It is usually brought in grade six). Veiling is a technique of painting whereby thin layers/washes of paint are applied on dry paper and the paper is allowed to dry between applications. There are several ways to go about this technique. Different sizes of brushes can be used, depending on the approach and the size of the paper.

Getting to know the paper

First the paper is taped onto the painting board. The paper can be taped on while wet, with special wide tape that stays down well on the board. Masking tape works quite well. Once the paper dries, it shrinks and becomes nice and flat and tight. When paint is applied, it softens, stretches out and 'bubbles up.' The paper can also be taped down while dry—it bubbles up to some extent, but this works just as well.

Controlling the brush

Layers of paint can be applied with a 1" brush, covering an area of paper quickly. The board is best held at an angle against the hip, or placed on a slanted desk, allowing the paint to create a drip edge towards the bottom edge of the stroke. Each next stroke takes up where the last stroke left off, picking up the drip edge as the brush moves along, until the wash is completed. The brush should not go over where the paint is already applied and wet. Any strokes repeated over a wet area will lift off the layer underneath and create a muddied effect. Once the wash has dried, another wash can be applied, overlapping the dried wash underneath, as desired. The gradual building up several layers of washes, with colors overlapping and strengthening in density and brightness, creates a stunning effect.

Short strokes

I decided to begin the veiling experience for my class with a smaller brush and small strokes, to allow for a gentle introduction and a more easily controlled way to introduce the students to veiling. With a ½" brush, small strokes are applied that can best be described as small 'wiggling fishes' of about one inch long each. The brush can be held so it goes flat onto the paper or at an angle to create a thinner stroke. When covering an area with these little strokes, different areas of color can be determined gradually. Slowly with the strokes beginning to overlap, a marvelous effect is created, overlapping colors whenever

desired. From a distance the painting gives an impressionistic effect.

Aerial perspective

Our first painting was a rolling hills landscape in different blues with a sunset or sunrise. With this landscape painting came really the first official lesson in aerial perspective. The students were ready for this and were able to actually see what aerial perspective is about in the rolling hills surrounding us, where the hills in the distance are a hazy light blue, becoming darker and denser as they come closer. They were able to follow that the trees closest to us are the darkest, and the further away they are the hazier they become.

Vertical strokes

After the landscape painting, some of the students had time to do another one, this time of a fire, with the brush strokes going up vertically in the direction of the flames and the smoke. This upward direction also creates a marvelous effect and affords much movement and fluidity.

GEOMETRY

The weeks of December are a most wonderful time to do Geometry. It is also a great time for the students to make gifts to take home to their families for Christmas. We learned how to construct a pentagram and make dodecahedron lanterns.

Painting the paper

First we painted two sheets of paper with lemon yellow, gold and orange colors. Then we made templates of the pentagram so that each student could trace the template 11 times. Each pentagram was scored from one midpoint to the other along each edge, so that the tabs left for gluing were triangular in shape. This resulted in the formation of a five-pointed star on the inside of each pentagram. Carefully scoring the tab edges before gluing, each pentagram was glued onto the next until the dodecahedron had its shape, leaving the top open. There were eleven pieces in all. It took a while for the glue to take hold with each side, so the students had to wait patiently while holding two edges together. Also, it was important for the students to be exact with creasing over the tabs. Any small deviations from the exact lines resulted in corners that did not match and fit well.

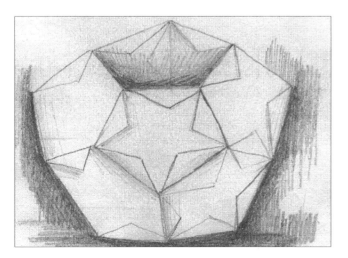

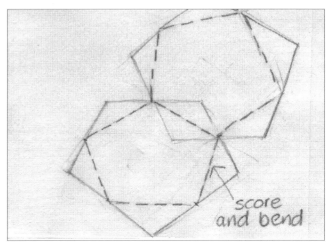

score and bend

GRADE SIX

We began the year with the study of Central and South America that afforded a wonderful opportunity to model Inca and Mayan sculptures out of clay. Each student modeled a statue of their choosing and worked with a considerable chunk of clay—about half a roll each, 6" diameter by 12" high. Some students chose to sculpt a Mayan temple with steps leading up to a flat top and smaller temples. Most students worked individually; only two shared a sculpture. Our display also included the students' individual study/reports on the countries they chose.

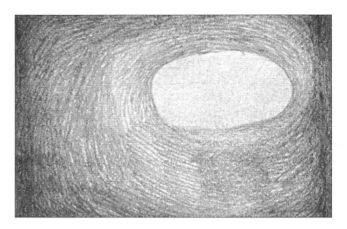

VEILING A CAVE

During our Mineralogy block we began a veiled cave painting with small ½" brushes. Veiling can be quite a challenge to coordinate since the paint has to dry between layers, especially when covering the whole page with one layer after another. So I chose to begin working on marionette puppets at the same time. This may sound rather ambitious but it worked well. While the students were waiting for their paint to dry, they needle-felted the heads of the puppets. Then, when the paint had dried sufficiently, they picked up their brushes again and painted another layer. In this way they alternated working on the puppets and the painting.

Many layers of paint

The cave began with a first layer of paint radiating inward from an imagined opening in the cave on the outside to the deep dark recesses. The opening was left white, a slightly oval shape. Each successive layer began ½" away from the previous one, each time extending all the way again to the periphery of the page. Each student could work at his own pace and was able to observe when his painting was dry enough for the next layer. When the outer layers were halfway to the outside edge from the cave opening, we all worked at the same time to form and shape the stalactites and the stalagmites and boulders on the cave floor.

Looking at each other's paintings

I felt that the students were ready to begin a friendly critique of each other's work. Up to

this point I had occasionally asked a student if I could hold up his/her work to show the class an example of how to proceed or to show a particularly good example. Having fostered an atmosphere of respect over five years, it was worth the risk to see how this would work. Could they be objective at this stage of development? Could their comments be fully constructive and not judgmental?

Giving the example

I began by reviewing how, in earlier years, I had often held up artistic work to give helpful comments, how we can all learn from each other, and how sometimes another point of view can be very helpful to the artist. We also talked about aerial perspective, what we had seen standing on the local mountain top and witnessed how the hills are darker when they are closer to us and become more and more soft and blue the further distant they are. Of course, as usual, comments could only be given when raised hands were recognized.

I began the critique by giving an example of what kinds of comments were appropriate. Could there be more stalagmites and stalactites? Was the composition balanced? Was the periphery dark enough? One by one the paintings were held up in front of the whole group, and many students offered constructive comments—all in all a very successful session. What was amazing was how all the caves showed more perspective when seen at a distance—rather than close up.

Completing the painting

In this painting only cobalt and Prussian blue were used. Prussian came into use only at the end of the process, to darken the innermost shapes at the back of the cave and to accentuate the shadows thrown by the boulders and stalagmites on the cave floor. Finally, at the end of the process, students were guided in painting the horizon stretching out in the distance out of the cave, showing a beach with the ocean and clouds in the sky above. For painting the horizon they used a very thin watery cobalt, light as can be, to accentuate the perspective of distance.

SILK MARIONETTES

We began creating our marionettes during and around this time—in preparation of a Christmas story for a December puppet show. I wanted to relate the puppets to our study of Mexico, Central and South America. We chose the Mexican story of how the poinsettia became the Christmas flower. This story was the right length and had wonderful content—as well as enough characters for all of the students to not only make a puppet but also perform.

Needle-felting the heads

Since all of the students were already very familiar with needle-felting, it was not long before they had made the heads. As we had only a finite amount of time available for this project, I pre-sewed the head coverings and the hands. I also pre-sewed the basic dress for each puppet out

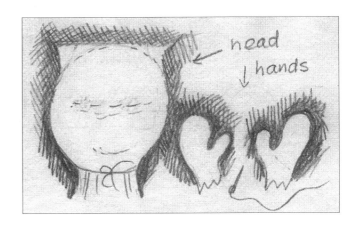

of white silk. Each student slipped on the head covering, established the neck and sewed the head onto their dress at the neck hole. The heads were covered with black hair according to the characters and sewn on to the head with black thread. Lifting up the dress to the top where the head was sewn on, shoulders were attached to the head. Hands were sewn on to the two arm ends of the dress with the thumbs up.

Who plays whom?

Parts were chosen after we had read the story. In my class over the years we developed a fair system of letting the names in the hat decide who was to get which part. If, for example, three students were interested in the same part, their three names were written on pieces of paper, crumpled up and placed in a hat or a basket. Someone with her eyes closed would pick out a piece of paper, unfold it and announce the 'winner.' We used this wonderful way of resolving a conflict numerous times.

Scenery

Since all 19 students had parts to play, the theatre that we used in grade five for the story of "Amahl and the Night Visitors" was too small to accommodate the whole class. A long time ago I had seen a marionette performance done without a theatre, without any sets, straight on the floor. We first thought to use the classroom as it would be so easy to just set up and take down in our own space. But the first time we tried it, we realized right away that we were too big for the

room and it would not work! Fortunately at short notice we were able to use a movement room that held no classes first thing in the morning.

Making do with little

I had a lot of silks left over from earlier grades' plays and nature tables and had also received some gifts of Mexican and Colombian material. We used these to make the floor set, along with a needle-felted nativity set of Mary, Joseph, a sheep and an ass. To add to the atmosphere and create a focus, we made a backdrop for four sets: the house, the church, the marketplace and the shrine. The class split into groups for each backdrop. The images were sketched out and then drawn with color pencils on painting paper. Once completed, the paper was pasted onto a backing of foam board.

To make it stand upright and balance, a piece of cardboard was attached to the back with two flaps leaning outwards on the floor. The students had to be careful not to bump their feet into the cardboard that stuck out about 6". Ultimately this arrangement worked, though it was hard for the students to always mind their feet and at the same time focus on what their hands were doing.

Rehearsals

There is an art to rehearsing, just like there is an art to everything else. Since all the students had parts, we placed chairs at the back for everyone, so those who were not on could sit with their puppets on their laps, waiting their moment

on stage. Just as in a play, it is important to give everyone a part so that they can feel included and not get too bored because they have to wait a long time to be a part of the show.

The final performances

We performed the show for all the grades, including the kindergartens, as well as the parents of the class. It was quite a sight to see all of the puppets 'on stage' at once during the procession to the church, with the candles all lit (we used fairy lights hidden under a drape, plugged in just as the church service was beginning). Having the play performed on the floor, meant it was quite hard for any children in the audience to see if they had other children in front of them. So ideally we had the first graders sit on the floor, fifth graders on chairs behind and seventh graders standing behind the fifth graders. The performance took only about 10–15 minutes.

MOSAICS

Mosaics are a wonderful art medium to work on during Roman History. There are several ways to approach this art of placing together small components to form patterns or create images. I had seen it done often with broken bits of colored eggshells or small squares of construction paper glued onto a white or black background. Having worked for many years with stained glass with middle school students, I chose to use small pieces of glass glued on to a piece of plywood for our project.

Purchasing materials

Having experienced how much effort it takes to score and cut glass, I purchased the glass far in advance of the actual time for the project. Fortunately my classroom budget allowed for this fairly expensive material. I also cut the plywood boards ahead of time, to help estimate the total area that needed to be covered by the little pieces of glass. I chose pieces of ½" plywood measured 12" by 16". It is always fun to go to a stained glass studio to browse through the many different colors and kinds of glass they have available. How much glass to purchase has to be an educated (or uneducated!) guess—and just what colors will be most popular. Sometimes a studio will have scraps for sale at a reduced price per pound—but there is not always the right assortment of colors you are looking for.

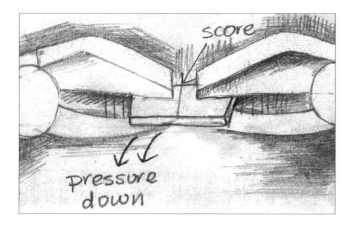

A rough estimate for each student's mosaic project expense is $15. This includes the plywood, glue, and the tools for scoring and cutting the glass. You will also need a scorer, some 'nippers' and some Elmer's glue.

Preparation

During the weeks of the Astronomy block we began to score and cut the glass. I bought a nice new scorer that proved to work really well. I had a couple of nippers left over from the 'old' days when I taught stained glass in the Manual Arts studio. With a couple pairs of goggles we were ready to cut the glass, two students at a time. I did almost all the scoring first.

How to work with glass

Glass is sharp and fun to work with. A few simple guides will help to avoid too much band-aid use. Goggles are essential to protect the eyes from wayward jumping pieces. (Regular safety

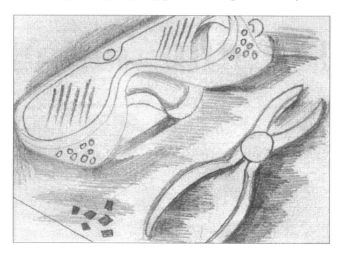

glasses will also work, but are not preferred.) The scoring is tricky and needs some practice. A steady hand is needed to score straight-line grids about a half-inch apart, depending on the kind and thickness of the glass. Once the glass is scored, it breaks fairly easily along the score. Some glass snaps at the slightest touch—other glass takes effort to break.

Breaking the glass

There are several ways to break the glass, one of which is the safest regarding avoidance of cuts. The glass can be turned upside down so that the score is on the underside, and the glass is tapped quite strongly on a hard surface at an angle. It will break in one or several pieces along scored lines. Or the glass can be gripped firmly with one nipper (breaker) at the score line with one hand, while, with the other hand, another nipper snaps off the other end of the glass. Lastly, there is yet another way, and this needs an experienced touch—otherwise it is easy to get cut. Hold the glass piece in the left hand, grip the other end with a nipper and bend the nipper downwards while at the same time putting pressure on the other side of the score and also bending that part of the glass down. Once you get used to this method, it is a quicker way to break a piece in two than coordinating two nippers to do the same thing.

Sorting the glass

As the glass pieces are cut, they need to be sorted immediately into containers according to color. Slowly the students can see the glass getting cut and being prepared for their use. Many students opted to cut during recess time, others cut glass in between doing other things in class during art periods. Meanwhile I also did a lot of cutting, at moments in between classes, while students were writing essays, and so forth. We had to put up a table at the side of the classroom for this, where everything stayed organized. The glass multiplied in the containers, and before too long we had all the glass cut and ready.

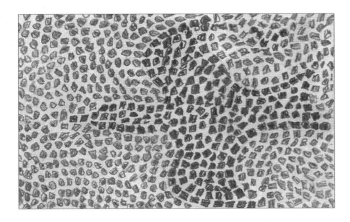

Trying out designs

Before going to the three-dimensional work, we began to get ideas for the project through working with pastels on black paper. During this exercise we discussed mosaics, their uses in hallways and floors of churches and other buildings, the different medium of glass, ceramic and stones that were used long ago, and how making forms with small squares gives a very distinct, unique look to the art. I wanted the theme of the designs to be connected to Roman times. Some students chose to do a Roman soldier or a sword, others chose more generic designs such as a waterfall fountain or fish in the water.

Pastels on black paper

Little squares of bright color are very effective on black or grey. The dark background makes the colors stand out. It gives the students a chance to check out the technique and to see that it is very different from detailed, carefully-done illustrations. Because it takes time to do

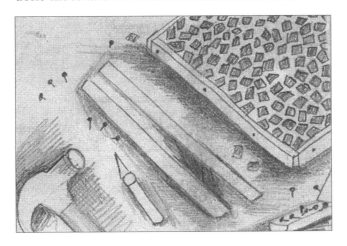

this painstakingly and neatly, we used the same size paper as the plywood boards. Even then, many students needed more than one period of Art to complete their paper mosaic. While they were working on their designs, I began edging the boards, one by one. I used balsam wood, purchased in three-foot long, three-inch wide strips, and cut the trim to the right edge height with an exacto knife (approx. ½"). Before nailing on the trim with small (¾") nails, I applied glue to the edges lightly. I used the knife to trim the edges to make the height of the edge flush with the height of the glass.

The final project

We needed several tables to provide enough room for all 19 students to work and have enough 'personal space.' I was on hand to cut anything that was not already cut—there were still some pieces left that were not scored or cut. I also needed to watch over everything in the beginning so that the small ½" pieces were glued no more than 1/8" apart. Once the pieces were glued and dried, it was time to do the final step—to grout.

Grouting

A 20lb. bag of sanded grey grout makes for an economical way to fill the cracks between the pieces of glass. This part of the project for many of the students was the most fun part. Most children like to get their hands in mud and they enjoyed spreading it around with their fingers and squeezing it into the cracks. Once they had cleaned off the excess, they could see the finished result come shining through! This is of course a dirty job and needed a lot of cleaning up afterwards. We did this job over the linoleum part of our floor so it was not too big a problem.

Uses of the boards

The boards can be hung as decorations in a room or used as hot plates at the dinner table. For decoration purposes, attach two rounded hooks at the top, and use a piece of strong wire to hang— the piece is quite heavy.

GEOMETRY

Learning about different forms of solids gives a wonderful opportunity to bring out the clay again. In addition to drawing them in their books, modeling solids in three dimensions helps students understand volume. After learning how to calculate the volume of a rectangular solid, first we drew seven solids in our books. In hindsight I would model the solids first, then draw them afterwards. The cube was the only Platonic solid, having six equal sides. This was a great introduction to the Platonic solids the students would study and construct in grade eight. Students enjoy looking forward and ahead to what they will do in the later grades.

All forms come out of a sphere

We began by modeling a sphere—a comfortable size, not too large for the hand, and not too large for the class budget! (Clay is expensive, and with 19 students it doesn't take too long to go through a box of clay!) After making the first sphere, we made a second sphere and turned that into a cube by pressing in the sides and making the edges and corners nice and sharp. It was clear that grade six students are ready and capable for this activity. After the cube came the rectangular solid, the triangular solid, a triangular pyramid, a square-based pyramid, and a cone. The students were very absorbed and enjoyed this activity. When they were finished, they each had a little 'village' of solids and all students managed to make the forms by themselves.

TISSUE PAPER 'STAINED GLASS'

Our classroom had wonderful south-facing windows, just the right shape and proportions for some medieval church-looking stained glass windows. For this project I chose to invite just the girls to work with me and see who would come during the Christmas break. It seemed daunting to even contemplate doing this project with the whole class, and fortunately just the right number of girls showed up to do the project—over a two-day stretch. The classroom really turned into a workshop as we used two long tables on which to work.

The template

Knowing how to make a template made the project doable, and even then it was tricky. A template of a window shape is best made with large sheets of paper taped together to the approximate size. Holding the paper up against the window, the edges are creased to fit exactly into the window-pane space. I could have allowed for an extra half inch, as the final product seemed to shrink, no matter how careful we were. Having made one template, I did not need one for the other window that was exactly the same, as we made one window at a time. (For two windows being made at the same time, you would need to make a second one.) With the template made, the 'structure' for the glass can begin. I chose to have an outside rim of 2" and inside structural lines of ½", made out of sturdy black construction paper. This looked like the right proportions.

Beginning with the outer structure, the strips of 2" black paper were laid out, overlapping about 2" for gluing together along the edges. (Heavy dictionaries were used to weight the strips down while they dried. They still curled up somewhat). This outer rim of the structure had

to be exactly according to the template. Once the outer structure was complete, the ½" strips were used for the upright support and the horizontal supports. Each horizontal support had a space of approx. 13" between them. Once the support structure was completed, we could begin the design.

What to depict?

The early stained glass windows in medieval times had mostly pictures from the Bible, as most people were illiterate and needed to see pictures to learn stories and legends. We chose Saint Francis and Saint Claire, one on each panel, facing each other. The girls worked together to come up with the design, and together we constructed the framework for the tissue paper. This was a long and exciting process. First the design was drawn onto the template, taken out from under the new framework for the panel, and hung up on the wall. Then we worked from the design to make the structure. We used mostly straight lines and a sampling of curves sprinkled throughout.

Time for tissue paper

Once the structure was completed, we could begin on the tissue paper. Tissue paper can be obtained in a set of many colors and is a wonderfully delicate material to work with. The most practical way to fit the pieces over the structure was to place the tissue paper over the structural lines, drawing lines in the middle of the lines, so the tissue paper would overlap by a quarter inch. Then the piece of tissue paper was cut along the pencil lines. To attach the piece only a very small amount of glue was needed all along the black edge of the lines. Excess glue would go on to the table underneath. We needed to check frequently that nothing was sticking to the table.

The whole panel was very unwieldy, and we could not pick it up easily and see what the results looked like. With some practice at delicate movements, we got the knack and could lift it carefully to take a peek. Large areas of one color, such as the robes of the saints, could be applied with large pieces of tissue paper, stretching over many black structure lines. This saved time. And at the end of the day when all participants were tired, saving time was of premium importance! Finally by 4 pm we were able to hang the first window—just before it got dark—so we could admire our work.

Making the matching window

With the first one under our belts, the second one was naturally easier to do. We didn't need another template; as the windows were identical, we just turned it over. We placed the design straight down on the template, to match the first one—so we did not need to draw it up either. We matched the color of the robes and used a similar color scheme. This panel also went faster, and finally we were able to complete the project. Both panels had indeed a church atmosphere, with the sun streaming through the colors. We were mighty pleased with the results!

How to know if something will work

When being creative, sometimes you have to take risks. I had in previous years made advent calendars, but they were on a small scale compared to these windows measuring 3' by 6'. The larger the window, the more unwieldy—you can count on that! But with some careful handling and good coordination, it proved to be doable. For the placement of the panel in the window, it is best to have some other adult help. I used duct tape to fasten it into place—nothing else will keep it up. (When I first hung them with regular masking tape, it was completely down and curled over itself when I came back to the classroom some days later.)

The costs

The risk is only the time you give towards it and the small cost of the material. The construction paper is fairly inexpensive, probably

ten sheets of 20" x 24" should be enough, as well as one set of tissue papers, assorted colors, and some glue. This is a huge project for very little cash outlay and a great way to transform the classroom for the second half of the year, giving the atmosphere of a church and bringing in lots of color.

MEDIEVAL KNIGHTING CEREMONY

This is a most wonderful ceremony with which to end the year, and there is much to do in preparation for this event. The knighting ceremony has been traditionally carried out in our school for many years, and each year we have hosted the Lake Champlain Waldorf School up in Shelburne, Vermont, for the games that follow. This year we invited the sixth grade to join us for the knighting ceremony as well.

The preparations

There are so many aspects to the preparation that planning has to begin long in advance, especially if a joint ceremony is planned. I met with the Lake Champlain sixth grade class teacher in March—two months ahead of the event that was to be held at the end of May.

We planned the preparations, as well as the schedules of events and the logistics of the overnight stay for the students from Vermont. Because it was to be a joint ceremony many aspects had to be coordinated for consistency, such as the tunics—they all needed to be the same.

Coats of arms

Each student chose three qualities to strive for as they prepared to become knights of the 21st Century and created their own coat of arms. Each quality was accompanied with a heraldic symbol, such as an eagle for leadership, a horse for readiness to serve, as well as certain colors. Each student prepared a small sketch of his or her coat of arms that then was translated into larger images for their shields. (Our guest class created banners from cloth.)

The shields

The shields were cut out of cardboard from a template and glued onto a second same-shaped piece of cardboard for extra strength. Students then painted a front and a back on painting paper, with the regular Stockmar watercolors, plain colors of their choice. These were glued onto the shields, and the edges finished off with their choice of colored duct tape, showing ¾" on either side. Once the painted papers were glued on, the shields were ready for the images. Many students made another template, this time about 2" in from the edges, and colored it with pencils in their choice of color. The chosen shapes were glued on top, like a collage, such as eagles, unicorns, and snakes, and also swords, axes, moons and stars.

Attaching the shields

With this completed, the shields were attached to pine sticks, 1" square and 6' long. Students decorated the sticks first with stripes of duct tape, their choice of color, before two holes were drilled, at the top and the base of the shield, and then attached/screwed on to the stick. The stripes on the stick really added a lot to the whole effect.

Different glues

By far the best glue to use is Yes! Paste, an odorless white paste that works really well in addition to not causing any wrinkling in the paper. The paste can be applied with the end of a ruler or a spatula for large areas, evenly though not thickly. Placing heavy dictionaries on top of the glued project will help to make the paste do the job. It never disappoints. It comes in small jars and is fairly expensive.

Tunics

We needed to make a new set of tunics and chose white, knee-length for the girls and white, thigh-length for the boys. The tunics were cut out and sewn on the sewing machine by the teacher. (Parents had recently helped with sewing costumes for the play, so this would have been additional work for them.) On each tunic front the students sewed a red cross, cut out of felt and tacked with small neat stitches of red cotton thread. Black sashes were made to go around the waist. Students wore black pants or tights underneath their tunics.

Garlands

The girls enthusiastically prepared garlands with a base made out of pipe cleaners artfully twisted and easily attachable at the back of the head. Ribbon was then twisted around the pipe cleaners for a lovely effect. Each student had a color theme. Additional ribbons hung down from the back.

Kings and Queens

Each class invited a king and queen of their choosing, people who had a relationship to the students, be they teachers or special friends of the class. In our case we had two sets, one for each class, who were magnificently dressed and sat up on the dais. There was just enough space for the four of them to fit in, sitting in chairs. They looked splendid! Both kings had swords; our King had made a special 'Excalibur' for the occasion out of wood, and afterwards he gifted it to the school for this ceremony for future classes.

The Queen had a basket of scrolls by her side, prepared by the teacher and students.

Scrolls

Scrolls were prepared in advance, once the striving qualities were determined by each student. Each student drew a small version of their coat of arms in a space provided. Then they were rolled up, and tied with red ribbon.

Invitations, place names

Invitations in calligraphy were sent out to all the students of the hosted school. This was a great opportunity for the students to practice their calligraphy skills. Place names were also prepared for the medieval feast to follow the ceremony. They were decorated gaily with medieval-themed illustrations.

The knighting ceremony

The ceremony can be held in a church, preferably a stone church with a medieval atmosphere and stained glass windows. We held ours in a small, local Unitarian church where there was ample but not too much room to allow for an intimate experience.

The schedule/program

- Leave for the church at 4 pm, already dressed, with the coats of arms.
- Have a go-through in the chapel so that the students are familiar with the order of events and how to organize themselves for the musical offering and the recitation of the oath.
- Line up in the anteroom and prepare for the ceremony to begin at 5 pm.
- Kings and Queens line up first and enter accompanied by stately recorder music.
- Teacher and knights follow and process down the aisle holding their coats of arms/banners.
- Coats of arms/banners are placed one at a time along the walls on either side of the seats.
- Students are seated and the ceremony begins.

Program

Welcome and introduction—host teacher
Story—guest teacher
Music by class
Recitation of oath by students
Knighting
Closing music and recession

The knighting

The knighting took place on an individual basis for each student. The Queen called up the student by his or her full name.

King: "We call you here to become a knight of the 21st century. Are you ready?"

Student replies, "Yes."

King: "Then please turn and state your chosen qualities that you are striving for!" (Student turns to the audience and states her/his three qualities.)

King: "Now kneel before me. I knight you now, and my wish for you is that you continue to strive and become a helpful and worthy Knight of the 21st Century." While speaking, the King slowly places his sword first on the one shoulder, then on the other as the Knight kneels before him.

King: "You may now turn to the Queen."

The Queen congratulates the lady or the knight, the student receives his or her scroll, returns to his/her seat, and the next student is called up.

After the knighting, the students were called up one by one to receive their coat of arms. When all of the coats of arms had been returned, all the students stood up in front of the Kings and Queens in the middle, facing the audience with their coats of arms. Then music signalled our exit, a slow recess down the aisle back to the anteroom.

If we were to have had just our own class, the knighting ceremony for each student could have been more involved, such as reading out a longer list of all the attributes and special things about each individual student. But with 42 students to become knighted, we had to keep it short and sweet for each one.

Medieval feast

After the ceremony there was a dance performed by the students, prepared by the movement teacher, after which we all filed downstairs for the feast. The coats of arms decorated the candlelit room and the finger food was medieval style, simple and delicious.

This brought the ceremony and our Medieval block to a celebratory end.

OATH
(to be learned by heart)

As a knight, I will do my utmost to:
Defend and aid the defenseless, weak or needy,
Be considerate of the feelings of others,
Think before I speak,
Keep an open mind,
Be grateful,
Have courage for the truth,
Be responsible for my actions and tasks,
Be respectful and understanding of others and
    myself,
Strive for what is noble and pure in thought,
Always and everywhere live with honor and be
    worthy of trust.
By fulfilling this oath, I will help to become a
    Knight of the 21st Century.

I told the students that their good deeds for the school and for home would continue in grade seven!

This knight _____
demonstrates the qualities
of: _____
_____
_____

GRADE SEVEN

With the study of Africa the tone for the year was set with a large board drawing showing this huge continent as the 'heart' of the world. Drawing the map of the world, showing Africa in the middle, also paved the way for the study of the ocean currents around the world and the study of the explorers later on in the year.

THE FIRST PROJECT

The first project that accompanied our study was painting the map of Africa in wet-on-wet watercolor. The land had an initial wash of yellow, followed by vermillion and blue for the mountains and green for the Congo basin, leaving the desert areas yellow. The continent was then surrounded by oceans, applied lighter in blue, round the outer edges of the continent and becoming darker towards the periphery of the paper. The result was a glowing continent in the middle of ocean blueness.

Individual research and reports

Each student took on researching an individual country and wrote a report done at home. This was accompanied by a clay model of

a piece of art from their chosen country, guided by a photograph from their research. Students worked with about 8lbs. of clay, a substantial amount to give them plenty to work with. The result on the display table, accompanying the studies, was a variety of pieces of African art including several masks, round pots, animal and human figures, as well as a tablet of hieroglyphs and a human head.

Working independently

At this stage of development, most students could work quite independently on clay modeling. There was still a tendency for some students to want to thump and beat up the clay, rather than to manipulate it with thumbs and fingers. They were encouraged to use their thumbs and fingers and whole-hand pressure rather than the slapping and punching gesture. This afforded a gentler instead of a more 'combative' approach to 'persuading' the clay to be moved around.

It is advisable to require the clay to be shaped into the desired forms with the hands only and to use tools only for details at the end. When tools are used from the beginning, much of the clay is 'taken away' (in little bits) to form the shape, usually creating a big mess and often wasting clay. When only the hands are used and the clay is maneuvered around, there is less clay taken off, less mess, and the student learns how to really manipulate the clay. The tools come in handy for folds and details that are hard for fingers to manage.

PAINTING

Our next project was to paint an autumn orchard scene, showing trees of different sizes in perspective, with autumn colors, leaves on the ground below, shadows on the trunks and the ground, with dappled colors indicating light coming through the trees.

The seasons

Painting trees in autumn affords a great opportunity to discuss nature and the seasons, relating them to different inner human moods and feelings. Once the paintings were completed, the students were asked to each write an autumn poem, describing the mood of their painting. The poems were written with decorations around the writing and displayed next to the paintings as a combined set of artwork.

Veiling

As with the cave painting in grade six, the students worked with watercolor on dry paper taped onto a board. Although they were guided in the beginning to establish the horizon and do a light lemon yellow wash from horizon down to the base of the paper, each student was free to choose her own composition as to where the trees were placed, their size and variety. The only requirement was that the trees had to be some distance from each other and receding into the background, adding to the perspective.

Techniques

The techniques used were both the wash with long strokes and the more impressionistic short strokes. Other than the initial ground wash of lemon yellow and the shaping of the trunks and branches, the short painted strokes were very suitable for the carpet of leaves on the orchard floor and for the bright leaves on the branches.

When viewing the completed paintings, it was evident that all the compositions were very different and yet shared the same medium and the same technique.

Viewing the work

There is an art to viewing work with students that encourages all students to feel good about their work. It becomes increasingly important that care is taken to ensure there is an all-round respect for the work of others, no matter what level of artistry. When the paintings were in the final phase, we practiced constructive critiquing with each student's work taking a turn at being looked at by the class. Looking at a painting from a distance, rather than close up, also allowed the students to see the elements of perspective more clearly and readily. Bringing in shadows onto the tree trunks and under the tree canopy, as well as behind the boulders placed here and there, was a considerable challenge for the students.

SHADOW PROFILES

This was a very popular project and marked the beginning of our work on drawing the human face. Drawing a human face with its proper proportions is a big challenge for seventh graders as they learn to observe keenly and draw what they see.

Working together

To begin with, each student 'sat' for his or her profile. With a white piece of paper (large enough to accommodate a slightly larger than full-sized head) hanging on the blackboard, each student sat sideways on a chair in front of the paper. A bright flashlight was balanced on a pile of books

at a distance to shine directly onto the student's profiled face. The shadow was traced all around the head with a pencil onto the white paper. Girls with long hair put their hair up in ponytails—this way they were more easily recognizable.

Cutting out the profiles

Each profile was cut out along the outer edge, then retraced onto black paper that in turn was cut around the outer edge. The last stage was to paste all the profiles onto a white background and to hang them up together in a group. The faces were pinned up on the wall with half the students facing left, the other half facing right. The students enjoyed seeing each other's profile on the walls, and parents tried guessing which profile belonged to which student. Some students were more easily recognizable than others. What makes a profile so recognizable was a great beginning to a discussion on how to tackle the drawing of a face and its features.

DRAWING THE HUMAN FACE, HANDS AND FEET

The face

Typically, a seventh grade student will draw the eyes too high up and on the forehead, so it is important for the students to begin this project by looking at the structure and proportions of a face. Beginning with the study of the eyes, they can be shown how there is a space/length of one eye between the two eyes, that the eyes are situated in the middle of the face and that

the tops of the ears are in line with the height of the eye-line. Seventh graders are also ready to learn, with careful work, how to make eyes look straight ahead into the eyes of the viewer. They are ready to see the space between the base of the nose, the lips and the chin, though for many it is an extreme challenge. With each exercise they improve their drawing skills.

Hands and feet

Hands and feet are great subjects for drawing but challenging. The students can position their non-drawing hand next to their drawing paper and sketch their own hand, or can learn from artists such as Dürer whose famous *Hands of the Apostle* (better known as "The Praying Hands") is a great example to copy.

When it comes to drawing the feet, it is fun to ask the students to take off their shoes and socks and put their feet up on their desks—an ideal opportunity to do something 'different.'

SCULPTING FIGURES IN CLAY

During the study of the Renaissance and learning about the monumental works of art by Michelangelo, sculpting in clay offers great opportunity for students to try their hand at forming a three-dimensional figure. A piece of clay 7" high x 5" in circumference stretches out for the most part into a 12" high figure, a good and workable size. Some of the figures had bases, others did not. Some were seated, others were standing. This time the students had tools available to work on final details, after first forming the basic figure.

Working from known works of art

Students were encouraged, but not limited, to working from photographs of famous Renaissance sculptures for inspiration. Examples of works chosen were seated figures on a base or standing figures that had a solid enough base. Recommendations included creating figures that did not have arms or legs too far extended from the body, due to the fragility of clay when it dries. Students were asked to look carefully at proportions, such as the size of the head and the length of the arms (and to learn from what they could see in the photograph). They were encouraged to keep turning their form around so

they could view it from all sides. Having studied cloth and folds in grade six, seventh graders were now able to go into the detail of forming folds in the medium of clay.

How to shape cloth draped over a figure

Portraying folds in cloth provides a unique challenge to the sculptor. When drawing folds, it is really a study about light not being able to reach inner recesses and showing the inner and outer parts of folds on a two-dimensional surface with light and dark tones. In sculpting, this inner and outer space of a fold becomes a real experience to the fingers and to the eyes: We can touch the inner recesses as well as see them. Some students used tools, others preferred to use just their fingers. In addition, folds can be rendered in such a way as to show dynamics of movement, rather than just straight hanging folds. It can be pointed out to the student that folds tend to be smooth and rounded, rather than sharp-edged and angular.

Showing gesture

During the middle school years, the ability to depict gesture begins to come into its own, though for many students figures drawn and sculpted still tend to be stiff and unmoving. For many the head still tended to be upright, and arms and legs showed minimum gesture. Some students turned the head sideways, or downward in a reverential gesture.

Sculpting hands and feet

During a Physiology block we modeled the hands and feet (keeping in mind that sculpting the head and bones can take place the following year during the eighth grade anatomy block). These two exercises followed along weeks after the initial drawing exercises. The assignment required that the foot be made the same size as their own foot. Once again the students took off their socks and shoes and put their feet up on the desks. They measured their own foot with a ruler and set to work. After some initial shaping many students preferred to place their foot on the floor and kneel down to do their sculpting right next to their own foot. It was challenging for them to observe that the toes were curved from the big to the little toe and that the heel was actually quite rounded, as well as seeing the roundness of all the curves of the foot.

GEOMETRY

Geometry in grade seven introduces calculation of circumferences and surface areas of circles, rectangular solids and other forms. Students are absorbing the differences between one, two and three dimensions and how to express the answers to their calculations as squared or cubed. While anticipating constructing the five Platonic solids in grade eight, we created mobiles of two-dimensional geometric shapes, using a great variety of colors and combinations.

Preparing the materials

First we painted large sheets of painting paper with washes of different colors and glued them back-to-back to create a two-sided colored surface about the thickness of poster board. The colors ranged from a mixture of red to yellow, blue to purple, yellow to green. Also available were various colors in construction paper, also strengthened by being glued back to back, using Yes! Paste, as always. Dowels, 1/8" thick for hanging, cotton thread, and duct tape completed the materials list.

Working in groups

Students were split up into four groups to work together. Each group had two dowels to work with and a quarter of the colored painted paper and construction paper that had been prepared. The team had to come up with a theme or a plan for their mobile that worked for each member of the team. There were no designated leaders (or chosen) and the groups were encouraged to practice consensus-building.

Construction guidelines

Only geometric shapes could be constructed, with a ruler and/or a compass, with variations of combinations of shapes glued on top of each other or inside each other. The shapes were to be drawn and cut out carefully on the outside, with the teacher being available to cut out any shapes inside (with an exacto knife) if required.

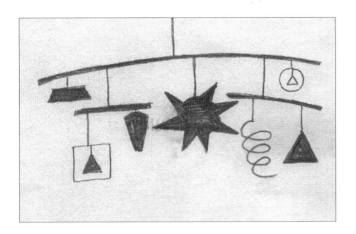

Hanging the mobile

With the shapes and forms so lightweight and in many cases delicate, hanging the mobile was a great challenge. Finding the balance between them all called for the use of tape over the spots where the threads were hung from the dowels. The end result was entirely satisfactory as the four mobiles hung over the students' desks and moved around elegantly with the slightest breath of air. Each group could see the results of their careful working together.

Compositions in pastels

Students next brought their geometry skills onto paper again, this time on the flat surface and done with pastel colors. They created a design on a smaller 8½" x 11" piece of paper using compasses and rulers only, this time superimposing shapes one over the other and learning to create a balanced composition.

The balance of colors

We studied the use of black and how it can be very effective when used in conservative quantities, as well as very dominating if used excessively. We also discussed how areas of white can give a sparkle to the overall work. Each student chose a color palette, with a minimum of six or seven colors used repeatedly throughout the piece. They worked on watercolor painting paper.

The versatility and limitations of pastels

Pastels are a marvelous medium with bright, beautiful colors. The colors can be applied richly and darkly and smoothed and moved around with fingers. The tones can move from dark to light and bring a quality that no other medium can compare with. However, trying to achieve sharp edges is a challenge with a chalky pastel stick. The medium is somewhat messy, and care has to be taken not to smudge the colors where clean lines and separation of colors are required.

Once the piece is completed, spraying the pastels with a fixative is advisable. This is best accomplished outside on a windless day and when the pieces can dry out quickly in the sun.

PERSPECTIVE

The study of perspective goes beautifully together with Renaissance history. Students can be shown many examples of Renaissance artists' works and how perspective begins to be used in not only the drafting plans of buildings but also in landscapes. These examples can be compared to earlier paintings such as by Giotto, where the background is often painted in gold without any depth perspective.

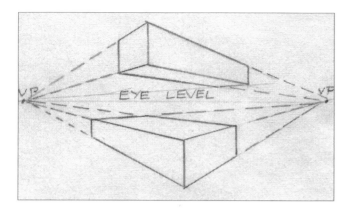

Beginning with the basics

Perspective drawing can be challenging for thirteen-year-olds. As an introduction, students can be led through basic four-part division, bisecting the space between two uprights with diagonals, such as the drawing of a gate with five posts. This fairly basic beginning exercise gives the students time to get used to drawing perpendicular lines from their horizons with their triangles and to draw their construction lines to the vanishing points. Lines need to be clean and crisp and exact, drawn with sharp pencils and a keen eye for precision. Once the gate has been constructed, students can add animals in front and behind and continue the fence to the left and right off to the vanishing points, adding color to the fields, and so forth.

Tree line into the distance

Four-part division with bisecting diagonals can then be applied to a tree line along a road, creating eight- or sixteen-part division. Fields and mountains can then be added to the landscape, and students can use their imagination by adding such things as cars on the road, even telephone lines on the other side.

Other exercises

There is a wide variety of exercises with one- and two-point perspective. One of the most enjoyable for the students is to create a cityscape and use their imagination to design different building shapes once they have practiced simple two-point perspective with blocks. In order for the students to be able to construct buildings that have three dimensions and actually take up 'real estate' on the ground, it is a good idea to bring in a box full of different-sized wooden blocks and position them together on a desk to show a city plan of, say, three 'blocks' with avenues in between. This will help them construct a good 'ground plan' before they draw up the perpendiculars and construct the roofs.

Showing the construction lines

It is helpful to have the students keep the construction lines and the ground plan lightly visible, to show how all the buildings actually take up space, before the city is furnished with color and details are added. Once the drawings are checked over, construction lines can be erased.

HOUSE PORTRAITS

This is a fun project to consider and enabled my students to apply their careful observation and beginning knowledge and skills in perspective to their own individual houses. Each student was asked to make a sketch of their own house at home and bring it in to school. The sketch included notes about color of siding, trim, doors, and roofs and landscape features such as shrubs and trees and foreground and background details. Students were advised to keep the angle of the view of the house simple, and many chose to do a straight-on view of the front of the house. For many this was challenging enough. Photographs of the houses were helpful for some to help with details and the overall perspective.

The final result

Students reproduced their original sketches onto good quality 9" x 12" sheets of 140lb. watercolor paper in light pencil lines with a ruler, keeping the lines crisp and upright. This was followed by applying light watercolor washes with the desired colors for the house and its details, followed by painting the foreground and background.

Framing

Framing a special project is an important consideration and makes a special gift for the students to give to their parents or friends. (This gift-giving coincided in my class with Mother's Day.) It is a lot of extra work for the teacher, but well worth it. A simple wooden frame with a colored matt border completed this project and the students managed their pieces to the best of their ability. As always with projects of any kind, some students needed a lot of guidance, others needed very little. Placed on display before going home as gifts, we had a wonderful collection of house portraits, and the students seemed satisfied with what they had accomplished.

GRADE EIGHT

Grade eight is a rich, culminating year in both academics and the arts. The students have experienced many years of artistic guidance and have been exposed to many different mediums and approaches during their seven years of learning about the world and all that life entails. At the age of fourteen they are very capable with their nimble fingers and increased developing ability for thinking about what they are doing. They have all become uniquely individual and are ready to explore more challenging projects.

ASIAN GEOGRAPHY

Having explored the African continent in seventh grade, this is a great year for 'traveling' even further and all the way through Russia to Asia, down Malaysia, along the Indonesian islands, and ending up in Australia and New Zealand. Along with the Geography block, two artistic activities to complement the study may be considered.

Portraits of Asian people

Students can apply all they have learned about the proportions of the human face to a final portrait of an Asian person. This can be combined with a research paper on a particular Asian country and its culture, with the emphasis on the people, particularly the natives such as the Maoris of New Zealand.

Color pencils lend themselves well to this project with the stipulation that the portrait needs to be life-size. Once the projects are completed and the portraits are ready, they make a marvelous collection and provide an interesting study on features and accessories such as hats.

JAPANESE SUMI PAINTING

The art of Japanese Sumi painting is very challenging, yet highly recommended. In preparation for guiding the students, it is a

all take time, as does the practice of holding the brush in an upright manner.

Resource

An excellent source for this activity is *Japanese Ink Painting Lessons in Suiboku Technique* by Ryukuy Saito (Charles E. Tuttle Company, Rutland, VT, and Tokyo). This gem of a book explains in detail what the art of Sumi painting entails and takes the reader/artist through making up the ink and the steps of creating the correct brushstrokes for a variety of illustrations.

A simple beginning

We began by practicing the elongated shapes of the bamboo stalks and its signature-shaped leaves. Students studied and very carefully observed the brushstrokes used and tried to make careful and deliberate strokes to imitate the master painting. Many repeated practice attempts were made before a final rendering could be considered. We practiced for many mornings for about twenty minutes at a time.

The final results looked good mounted on a black or dark grey background to complement the ink color. Once the bamboo was accomplished, many students also enjoyed painting a mandarin duck or little sparrow-type birds. Time restrictions did not permit practice of some other more challenging paintings such as apple blossoms or a typical Japanese house in a landscape setting.

good precaution to have lots of newsprint pads for practice. It is most definitely not a one-time activity, but needs to be practiced for a considerable length of time with care and much thought. The grinding of the ink on the stone and the preparation of the various tones of black

Materials used

Sumi painting requires special paint, brush, and rice paper that can be ordered online. The brush is delicate and has to work well by coming to a point when wet, otherwise the strokes will not come out as intended or desired. Rice paper is a very thin paper that can be obtained in different colors. It is very absorbent and if a brush has too much ink on it, the ink spreads out too much beyond the intention of the brush stroke. Many students preferred to use the newsprint they had practiced on or a grey, rough-surface paper similar to construction paper that was not so absorbent and did not let the ink bleed out as much.

ANATOMY

The skeleton lends itself very well to sculpture in clay. Having a life-size skeleton available in the classroom is essential; it would be challenging to attempt this study from just illustrations. Aside from this, students get a 'kick' out of having a skeleton in the classroom at this age. We called ours 'Charlie' and he was very popular.

Creating the space

We set up a long table in the middle of the classroom, easily accessible to all students, and covered it with a white cloth and a thin layer of see-through plastic. Seated in groups around with boards and clay, students were assigned different parts of the skeleton. Two students were assigned to work on the skull, five on the vertebrae, two on the pelvis, two on the collar bones and pairs of students on the limbs.

Structural support

The elongated clay bones for the arms and legs needed structural support so that they were less likely to break while going through the drying process, as well as giving support throughout the shaping. Wooden dowels ¼" and of appropriate lengths are suitable for providing this central support. Students wrapped the clay around the dowel and built up the shape gradually. As the clay dried, it began to shrink in all directions and needed some patching up in some places.

Laying out the skeleton

As the bones were completed, they were positioned on the table in the correct anatomical places. We had decided earlier in discussions on the skeleton that the ribs were too thin and delicate to be created out of clay, so we had to leave them out. The pelvis was sculpted in a flat shape with some of the curves and sculptural aspects of the form compromised to accommodate the skeleton's horizontal position on the table. The skull was hollowed out to show the shapes on the inside.

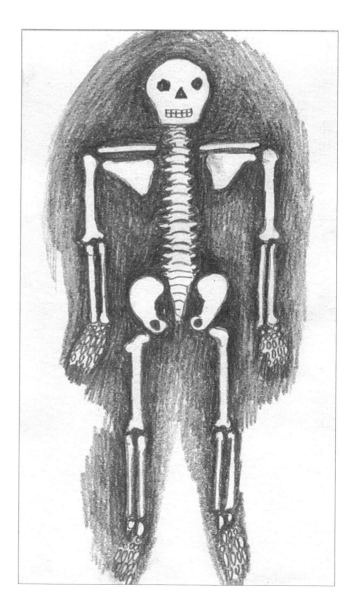

CREATING A LIKENESS OUT OF CLAY

Another great project for the students was to sculpt heads/busts of each other (as opposed to sculpting themselves). This is a complex undertaking that needs lots of space and time allowed to carry out the project in a satisfactory and manageable manner. The best time to do this might be before or after the skull has been shaped during the anatomy block. However, this project can be done during any other block independently of any subject being studied.

Partners

Partnering the students to create each other's portraits is fairly tricky but doable with some planning and forethought. Each student will need to feel good about making this for another student to take home. Since this project may be challenging to many, the teacher needs to be available to help where help is needed in order for everyone's sculpture to be a success.

Source

A great source for this project is *The Portrait in Clay* by Peter Bruno (Watson-Guptill Publications, New York). It is a well-written, complete step-by-step guide to sculpting a portrait out of clay.

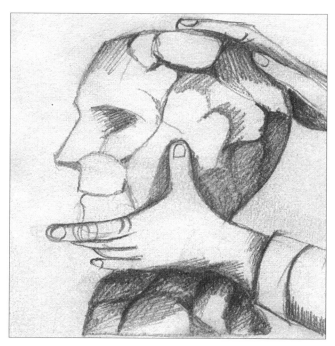

I copied some of the pages and hung them on the board for the students to view and refer to. This was particularly helpful for details such as the eyes. Students could also use the book for reference whenever they needed. (You can expect the book to get covered with clay fingerprints.)

Materials used

Plywood, curtain dowels, flat screws, felt, clay, small sculpting tools, hollowing tools. Beginning with the first indications in the book's instructions, 12" x 12" x ¼" boards of plywood were prepared, one for each student. A hole was drilled through the middle of each board. The curtain rod was cut up into 10" sections and each piece was attached to a board with a screw. (Drill a hole into the rod before attaching so that the screw can fasten more easily.) Felt was glued onto the base of the plywood board so that students using the boards on their desks could turn their boards around without scratching the desks tops.

Using clay

This project required a considerable amount of clay; allow for at least 12lbs. per head sculpture to start, knowing that from each hollowed-out head approximately 3lbs. will be retrieved at the end. Each student began as indicated in the instructions by pressing slabs of rectangular pieces of clay around the armature (curtain road dowel) and so building up the shape of the head. Make sure the initial building-up of the clay is supervised as much as possible, to make sure that the armature ends up covered thickly enough on all sides of the head. This is important because when the head is hollowed out, it can be tricky trying to pry the armature out if it is situated too close to the face. Equally important is for the students to pack and blend in the clay so that the clay base is firm and tightly packed.

Shoulders as support

Before beginning the features, the shapes of the dome of the head, the neck and the shoulders need to be carefully checked for size and proportion. The students had fun using rulers to measure each other's heads. The shoulders need to stretch out to the edges of the board, and be at least 4" wide so as to support the head. In a few cases, the neck was wobbly (despite the armature) and had to be carefully tended over the days, to make sure the head did not lean too far forward or too far back. Before the hollowing out process lightened the weight, some of the

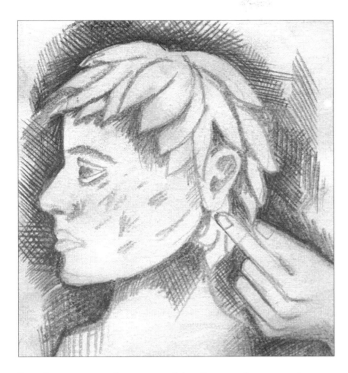

heads were top-heavy and had a tendency to lean back, threatening to wobble backward and fall down. In these cases we broadened the base of the shoulders on the width.

Features

Finding the level of the eyes and hollowing out spaces for the eyes is the next step. It is frequently a challenge to place the eye-level more in the middle of the face than higher up, and of all the features, the eyes take the most time and

effort. Students can now practice and apply all they have learned about the proportions of the face. It is advisable to suggest they bring the nose and ear shapes out of the clay rather than adding them (as shown in the book) to lessen the risk of the separate pieces not being adequately attached and blended in.

The profile

Careful study of the profile and making sure the nose resembles that of the student's is paramount to achieving a likeness. Frequently the indent above the bridge of the nose was omitted resulting in many of the students having 'Roman' noses.

Hair mass

The illustrations in the book show the whole process of adding the hair mass as well as indicating the neckline. The hair mass is also critical to being able to achieve a likeness. The mass should be an average of ½" or 1", depending on the mass of hair of the student. Textures and indentations were added for curls and wavy locks.

Help with the final completion

'Doing the rounds' from desk to desk works quite well, giving words of encouragement to each student. Advice about some changes needed goes a long way. Some students struggled to get

the basic head shape; measuring from head to chin with a ruler helped. Partners needed to sit together in proximity so that they were always able to check features and measure distances.

Students helping students

I had two students who were particularly adept at this project and who completed their busts before most of the others. They were able to help others achieve as much of a likeness as possible, by going round and helping particularly with the fine-tuning of facial features.

Hollowing out

The heads were very top-heavy and benefited from being hollowed out to make them lighter, as well as saving on clay. Hollowing out is a procedure that needs to be well supervised, to make sure not too much clay is removed. Removing too much clay could jeopardize the features or the roundness of the head while the clay is still soft.

Taking the head off the board

Take the screw out of the base of the board and place the head upright on the table. Taking a wire cutter, slice off a section of the scalp diagonally, high enough not to cut into the armature, and carefully place it to the side. Leaving a minimum of one-inch thickness on the outer sides, carve the clay out of the inside with a hollowing tool around the armature as far down as can be reached. The armature will be stubborn and reluctant to be moved. Next, place the head on its side gently and carve out the base, again leaving more than an inch around the edges, until the armature is finally freed. To make the base as solid as possible, replace some of the carved-out clay to fill in the space and solidify the shoulders but leave an opening.

Completing the project

Turn the head the right way up and gently replace the top of the skull in the same position before it was sliced off. Pinch the edges together gently and hide all evidence of the 'surgery' by smoothing over the hair. This has to be done delicately so as to not dent in the head. The boards can be re-used for working with the Platonic solids.

PLATONIC SOLIDS

This is the culminating geometry block at the end of eight years of elementary school. Students experience the five regular forms in both solid clay forms and hollow paper construction. Students have experienced sculpting solid forms before, such as the cube in grade six, and can now try their hand at more complex forms such as the dodecahedron and icosahedron, striving all the while for perfect symmetry. Some students will remember the forms from their last experience and find that they can make sharper edges and crisper vertices and enjoy the challenges of these more complex forms.

Sculpting the five regular solids

It is advisable to sculpt the Platonic solids out of clay before constructing them out of paper. This introductory experience gives weight to the solids and allows the fingers to explore the symmetry while turning the clay around in the hand, constantly changing the angle of view and allowing for full manipulation of the fingers. While it is good to have a board on the desk surface, it is beneficial to encourage the students to work the form in their two hands only, rather than banging the clay against the board or using the board as a tool.

Beginning with a sphere for each solid

Each student began by forming a sphere in the hands from a slab of clay. Start with the simplest form of the tetrahedron, asking the students to imagine a four-sided figure with equilateral triangles that are exactly the same. It will be a challenge to get perfect symmetry so that the solid looks the same from any angle viewed and has flat faces that have no concavities, straight edges that do not bulge out or cave in, and crisp vertices that come to clean corners. Move on through to the more complex forms: the cube, octahedron, dodecahedron, and finally the icosahedron.

Showing examples

It is most likely necessary to have examples to show when it comes time for sculpting the dodecahedron (twelve faces of five-sided pentagons) and the icosahedron (twenty faces of equilateral triangles). Even with an example in front of them, some students will find these many-sided forms overwhelming.

Constructing the nets

Use fairly heavy-weight painting paper to construct the patterns, again beginning with the tetrahedron, following the same order as with the clay modeling. Students will need to exercise great precision with sharp-pointed pencils, carefully measuring, adding the tabs in the correct places and accurately cutting in order to be able to have well-fitting three-dimensional paper forms in the end. Folding the edges and the tabs against a ruler is essential for clean, sharp folds.

Taping versus gluing

It is preferential and more time-effective to tape the forms on the inside rather than using glue. It creates less mess, does not take time to dry and is just as strong. Taping is also recommended on the outer edges to strengthen the form and to make it more permanent. Strings for hanging were attached by tape on the inside and allowed to hang out of any one of the vertices.

Decorating

Decorating the forms with brightly painted watercolor paper prepared in advance completed the projects. Each student needs two pieces of painted paper, using different color combinations for a varied effect. This completely covers any evidence of tape, and again requires very careful cutting so that the edges meet neatly and no tape is peeking through. The paper can be cut out with a little allowance, attached with fairly thickly applied Yes! Paste and then the excess carefully trimmed away.

PAINTING INSPIRED BY THE MASTERS

If time and opportunity allow, grade eight is a wonderful year for students to paint after a master. After eight years of steadily learning and working in many different mediums, it is wonderful to see how capable they have become. They are ready to tackle a challenge and to be inspired by famous artists. Important considerations are which work of art and artist works best for each student so that they can all have a successful experience. You want them to feel proud and satisfied with what they can accomplish, each in his or her own unique, individual way.

Choosing artists

A teacher who has been with the students for many years is intimately knowledgeable of their capabilities and can intuit what work of art would be best suited for each of them. Connecting to the study of modern history lends itself to considering the Impressionists and modern painters. In addition, the free method by which masters such as Van Gogh and Monet painted lends itself perfectly to the blossoming artistic talents of fourteen-year-olds. The subject of light shining on objects and how light is perceived in nature adds to the suitability.

Choosing a medium

Having worked extensively in watercolor for many years, and having explored different mediums such as pastels and charcoal in the previous middle school years, students were ready for an introduction to oil paints, especially since most of the artists chosen painted in oils. Impressionists painted straight from the palette to the canvas, often mixing the paints on the canvas itself, or painting pure colors in small brushstrokes that overlapped and integrated. This type of free painting renders itself very suitable for the students as they worked with a master's copy next to them.

The goals

The aims for this project were primarily enjoyment and a feeling of success, as well as some freedom for artistic license. The best way to ensure their enjoyment is to allow the students to choose what inspires them and what images they are drawn to within the parameters set by the teacher. Preparing some examples of possibilities is helpful to the student, rather than leaving the field too wide open. I steered them away from anything too modern that had a complicated psychological aspect to it or seemed inappropriate. Students were able to select a great variety of paintings representing artists across a fairly wide spectrum, ranging from Van Gogh to Kandinsky, all within reasonable chance of success. The paintings were meant as inspiration and no student was expected to 'copy' it exactly. The most important aspect was that they could learn from the artist and, if further inspired, even add something to it of their own. One student changed the color of a little boat from brown to red since the general colors were browns and greys. This livened up her painting and made it uniquely her own.

A feeling of accomplishment

Ending their eight years of artistic work with this experience was invaluable. Painting straight onto the canvas was enjoyed by all the students, without exception. Just a bit of guidance now and then was all they really needed, so they felt they had successfully accomplished the painting on their own. They were proud to complete their paintings and see them hanging on the wall.

THE EIGHTH GRADE PLAY

The culminating play at the end of the eight-year elementary school journey is an important moment in time in many aspects. It marks the end of all the plays through the eight years and gives the students an opportunity to recognize how much they have learned and how far they have

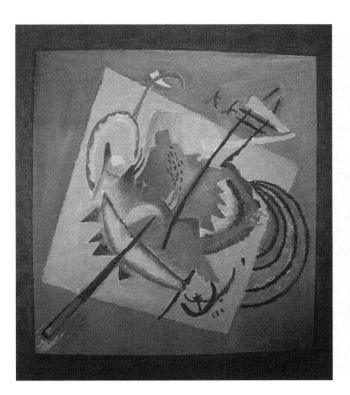

come in their development to be able to express themselves in front of an audience. It would take a whole chapter to do justice to this experience and task for both students and teachers. What follows will need to suffice as a small window into the whole undertaking.

The school culture

Depending on the culture of the school, Shakespeare may be a tradition or an occasional choice. At our school a great variety of plays have been performed over the years: *Peter Pan, The Wizard of Oz, Fiddler on the Roof, The Sound of Music, The Secret Garden, A Dime a Dozen, The Lion, the Witch and the Wardrobe, David Copperfield* and popular Shakespeare plays such as *Much Ado about Nothing, A Midsummer Night's Dream,* and *The Tempest.* What you end up choosing as a teacher and a class much depends on the constellation and talents of the students in the class and the help that is available to you for costuming, set design and, most of all, directing.

The selection process

The process of choosing what play is best suited to the class can begin before the seventh grade year has ended. Our process began when the grade before us had just completed their performance of *Much Ado about Nothing* at the end of the year and we had a discussion on Shakespeare, to whom the students had been introduced in their language block earlier in the year. The students remembered seeing *The Tempest* performed some years back and many were enthusiastic about this play. The decision for this play was made by majority vote, with the approval of the few who had other ideas.

Making a decision at this time allowed for editing the play in the summer to make it a reasonable length and child-friendly. Fortunately I had the help of a grandparent of one of the students in the class, a retired former high school literature and drama teacher, who was also available to help direct the play and work with the students' diction and gestures.

The Shakespeare block

It is a tradition in many schools to study Shakespeare in grade eight, independent of whether one of his plays is chosen. But if the class is heading in this direction, it is advisable to have the block on Shakespeare at the beginning of the year, maybe as a second block at the end of September. This allows for a process of casting and getting excited and enthusiastic about the play to begin early on, and enough time to do some final editing of the script. In addition to the life of Shakespeare, the class can learn about the history of the theater and how eventually the Globe was built once Shakespeare's company, The King's Men, found a home rather than travel around from place to place. This is important for their understanding of plays in the time of the 16th century, as well as for putting on a Shakespeare play in the modern age.

BY ELISE DRAPEAU

Reading *Romeo and Juliet*

We read this play, one of the first plays Shakespeare wrote, as a warm-up to our reading of *The Tempest*, one of his last plays written. Shakespearean language is hard for modern students to understand and to become familiar with, and the reading practice is invaluable. Students can begin to get an understanding of how the lines were composed and how they flow with punctuation and hyphens, as well as 'get in their ear' the strange-sounding words typical of the time.

Casting the play

Over the years my students had been given opportunities to 'have a say' in the casting of the roles. So once again, each student was asked to put forth their three choices, and they were assured that they would get one of their choices. Over the summer I had gone through the play extensively and already figured out who would be well-suited for which role and how it might all work out. It was clear that some students were ideal for certain roles and I put together a 'suggested' list of roles. I revealed this list before they wrote their choices on the pieces of paper, just before we began to read *The Tempest* and decide who would read what.

The power of suggestion is strong

Most of the students were enthusiastic about the role I had imagined for them, with a few exceptions. Knowing how important it is for all the students to be happy and satisfied about their parts, I decided to double-cast the play, so that all students could have one of their choices. With a play as extensive as a Shakespeare play, I could not imagine even attempting it without the enthusiasm of every single student. It turned out that there were only three roles that several students wanted, so each cast was fairly similarly composed except for three exchanges of roles.

The set

As with all other aspects of an eighth grade play, it is very important for students to feel their ideas and contributions are valid and important. Designing the set is an integral part of student involvement. Preparing the way for this is advisable. I worked on the set design over the winter break, figuring out all the exits and entrances so as to utilize all the space available on stage, and, as a teacher, to be as familiar with the details as possible. (I had created a mini auditorium/stage complete with exit and entrance doors as well as steps leading down to the audience.) I asked the students if they were interested in seeing the set I had imagined for the play, as I was ready to take it all down so that they could start fresh with their own ideas. They all wanted to see what I had come up with. The students who signed up for the design sessions were split into two groups and worked separately from the rest of the class. Each group came up with some additional ideas and embellishments that were incorporated into the overall design.

Keeping it simple

Designing a set is one thing, but producing it is quite another. Much depends on what parent help is available in the weeks before the play as well as the 'tech' weekend before the week

of performances. Many details can already be prepared beginning six weeks in advance of the final week, depending on available space to work in and to store props. In addition, during the month of rehearsals, there may be other events on stage that have to be circumvented. It can all become very complicated and keeping it simple and manageable according to the available helping hands is well advised. Students can help wherever they can, being very capable at this age.

Organizing costumes

Students will enjoy making sketches of their characters with some guidelines as to the typical dress at the time the play was written. Some costumes will doubtlessly need to be sewn from scratch, others can be borrowed or rented, depending on 'borrowing availability' and the budget allocated for the play. Color coordination of costumes can be worked out once the sketches are completed. Keeping the set simple also gives the costumes a chance to really show to their best advantage.

Music and lighting

Music can be an integral part of a play. Piano or harpsichord, percussion instruments, recorders—all instrumental sounds enliven the atmosphere, help with the transitions from one scene to the next and 'bind' the entire experience into one whole. Lighting creates atmosphere and is equally integral, creating emphasis and mood where necessary and appropriate. Lighting brings the set to life, as well as helping accentuate other areas off stage when possible.

Learning lines

This is a vital part of the whole organization of putting on an eighth grade play. Students need enough time to understand their roles, to become immersed in the play and to learn their lines by heart. Before the students begin to practice their lines, it is important to review the play again, this time in depth as a whole class, going over the exits and entrances, the pauses and the flow of the lines. A beginning understanding of how their

own characters should speak and act on stage is really helpful to set the students off on the right track. Four weeks plus a week of vacation were allotted to this learning and practice process. Students were expected to go over their lines each night before going to sleep, to help with the memorization process.

Editing the play

Shakespeare's plays tend to be over two hours long. Some roles have many lines, some have just a few. To bring this more into balance and to shorten the performance time to about a hour and a half at the most, it is important to edit/cut lines wherever possible without eliminating any essential parts of the story. It may also happen that lines have to be cut because one student or another may not be capable of learning their designated number of lines.

Beginning rehearsals

Warm-up speech exercises are crucial for beginning rehearsals each morning. Time is of the essence and the weeks need to be carefully organized to maximize time and energy as well as keep the enthusiasm ongoing. Working on gestures and how to project to the audience needs to be a big part of learning the lines, the cues and the interactions with the other actors.

Blocking

Working out exits and entrances and where the action takes place on and off stage is a major undertaking. Depending on the space available, the aim is to make the play as smooth-flowing as possible, to vary the comings and goings of the actors and to utilize all the possibilities the space allows—including acting in the middle, side, back or around the audience. This basic blocking should take place before beginning rehearsals, just to give a foundation for the first week. Gradually things will fall into place and adjustments and changes can be made as the rehearsals get into full swing. A beginning and an ending group reflection each day on how things stand and what is to come are essential to the process. Students need continual encouragement, as for many this is a considerable undertaking.

Support for the teacher

It is extremely helpful and advisable to have another person co-directing or as a right-hand person, who is preferably familiar with the play and with teenagers. This task is large enough even for two! If a co-director is not possible, then

a person who can help with production can be invaluable. To keep track of all the details, such as the props, is formidable, no matter how hard one tries to keep things simple. Help backstage for final rehearsals as well as the performances is essential. All these elements and more are the ingredients that make it possible to take on this formidable rite of passage as the students say farewell to their elementary school years.

> *Ye elves of hills, brooks, standing lakes and groves,*
> *And ye that on the sands with printless foot*
> *Do chase the ebbing Neptune and do fly him*
> *When he comes back; you demi-puppets that*
> *By moonshine do the green sour ringlets make,*
> *Whereof the ewe not bites, and you whose pastime*
> *Is to make midnight mushrooms, that rejoice*
> *To hear the solemn curfew; by whose aid,*
> *Weak masters though ye be, I have bedimm'd*
> *The noontide sun, call'd forth the mutinous winds,*
> *And 'twixt the green sea and the azured vault*
> *Set roaring war: to the dread rattling thunder*
> *Have I given fire and rifted Jove's stout oak*
> *With his own bolt; the strong-based promontory*
> *Have I made shake and by the spurs pluck'd up*
> *The pine and cedar: graves at my command*
> *Have waked their sleepers, oped, and let 'em forth*
> *By my so potent art. But this rough magic*
> *I here abjure, and, when I have required*
> *Some heavenly music, which even now I do,*
> *To work mine end upon their senses that*
> *This airy charm is for, I'll break my staff,*
> *Bury it certain fathoms in the earth,*
> *And deeper than did ever plummet sound*
> *I'll drown my book.*

And so, with these words of Shakespeare (*The Tempest*, Act V), this chapter ends.

Our journey is now complete. It has been rich and rewarding in innumerable ways. Being able to share it with others is a privilege, knowing that so many projects will pass through children's hands to augment their academic learning. Blessings on your journey!

Main Lesson Book Binding

Materials needed:
- Spiral-bound drawing pads or main lesson books with cover and cardboard backing
- Tapestry needles, big, not sharp
- Dental floss—yes, dental floss! It is strong. ...
- Yes! Paste (Order on the internet; it is fairly expensive.)
- Dowels: not too narrow (¼") and longer than the spine height
- Large binder clips
- Painting paper
- Drill—used if main lesson books do not have holes; thin drill bit but large enough to make a hole for the needle to pass through
- Drill template, only used if main lesson books do not have holes
- A large cutter to cut painting paper, or any other set-up you can find to keep the cuts straight

Cover: two pieces of painting paper glued onto two pieces of cardboard
Insert: student's work
Spine: a slim piece of painting paper that holds the covers together

Follow the directions carefully. If in doubt, practice on a thin little book first, to get the hang of it, rather than your child's precious main lesson book. Make your own notes so that you can remind yourself of the process as you do the real thing.

DIRECTIONS
(See illustrations on the next two pages.)

Cover paintings
Each student paints two paintings, one for the front of the main lesson book and one for the back. The paintings must be at least one inch larger on each side the book, with extra to spare for the additional spine covering, as shown in the drawings. If the paper used for painting is just large enough to cover the book pages with an inch all round, make a separate painted paper for the spines. Make sure the child's name is on each painting. Think about the direction of the painting and recognize that representational paintings may not work well because not all of the painting will appear on the book cover. Press on a flat surface for at least 24 hours.

The cover
The cover of the bound main lesson book consists of two pieces of cardboard glued to the painted outside covers. Use the cover and back of the original main lesson books for gluing onto the inside of the cover. (When taking out the coil, keep the back and front, and discard any unused pages in the book.) Cardboard sold in stores comes in large sheets and is tricky (but not impossible) to cut. Use a triangle for 90 degree accuracy (such as the ones used for geometry drawing), a long ruler and an exacto knife with a new, sharp blade for the cutting. Cut the cardboard the same size as the main lesson book pages.

If the original main lesson book was not spiral-bound and has stapled pages instead, take out the staples and drill the holes using a template made out of ¼" plywood. (When drilling through the template onto the pages of the book block, place a piece of wood underneath so you don't drill into the table.)

You can embellish the inside of the cover once everything is completed, by gluing an additional piece of paper over the cardboard so that it looks nice when you open the book. The child's name could be on the inside cover left hand side.

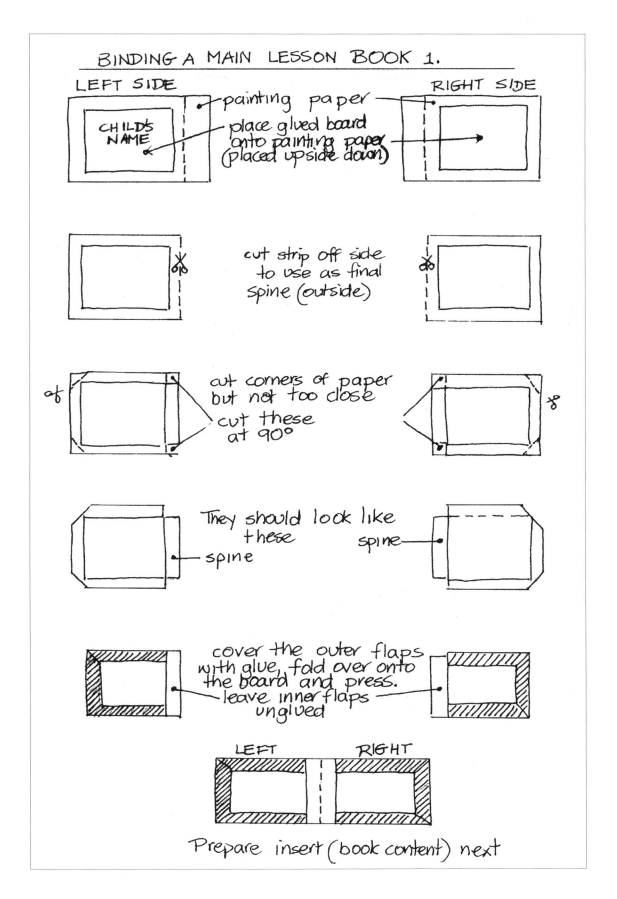

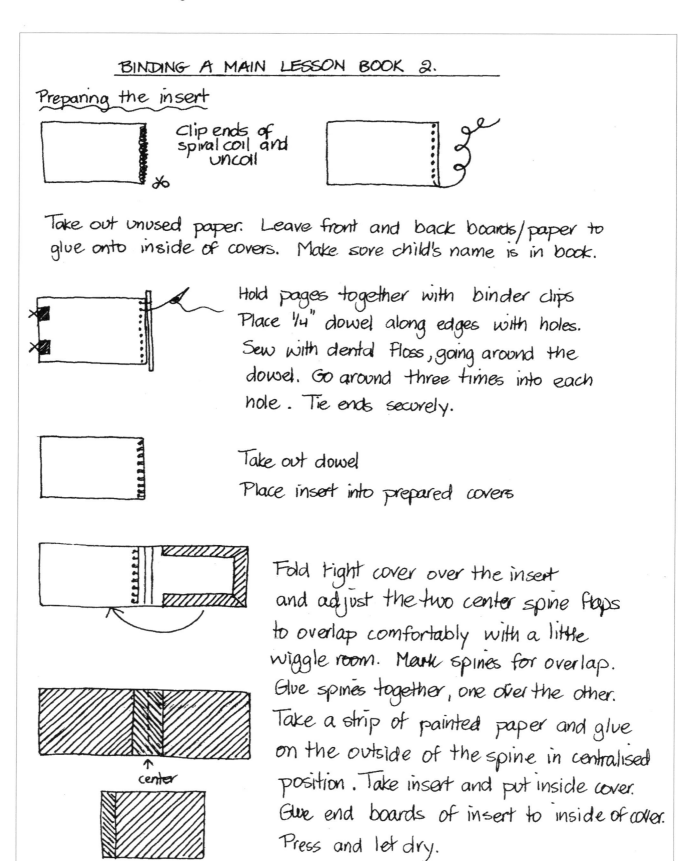

BINDING A MAIN LESSON BOOK 2.

Preparing the insert

Clip ends of spiral coil and uncoil

Take out unused paper. Leave front and back boards/paper to glue onto inside of covers. Make sure child's name is in book.

Hold pages together with binder clips
Place ¼" dowel along edges with holes.
Sew with dental floss, going around the dowel. Go around three times into each hole. Tie ends securely.

Take out dowel
Place insert into prepared covers

center

Fold right cover over the insert and adjust the two center spine flaps to overlap comfortably with a little wiggle room. Mark spines for overlap. Glue spines together, one over the other. Take a strip of painted paper and glue on the outside of the spine in centralised position. Take insert and put inside cover. Glue end boards of insert to inside of cover. Press and let dry.

Painting the Hebrew Myth of Creation

Day One: Let there be light!

Day Two: separation of air and water

Day Three: the land below and the first plants

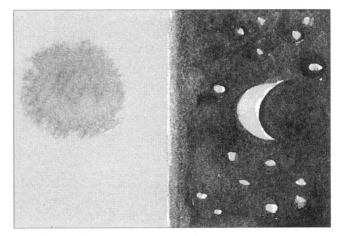

Day Four: the sun, moon and stars

Day Five: the fishes and the birds

Day Six: humans and animals

VEILING THE CAVE

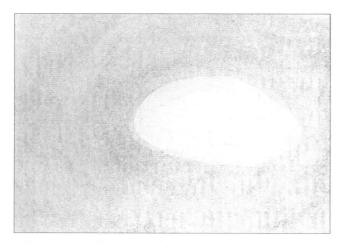

1 Beginning the cave: the opening

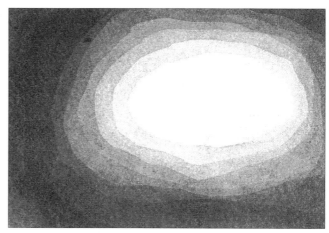

2 Completing the layers

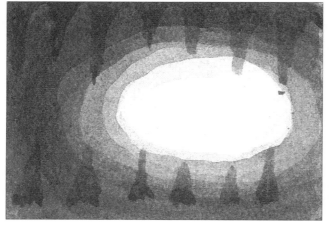

3 Building up the stalagmites and stalactities

4 The outer periphery rocks and boulders

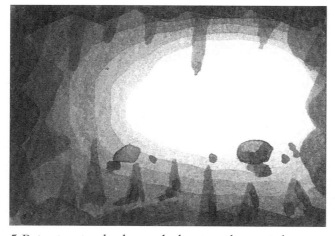

5 Bringing in shadows, darkening the periphery

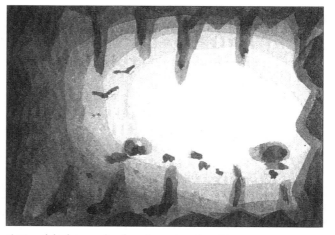

6 Establishing the horizon in the distance

Navajo Loom Instructions

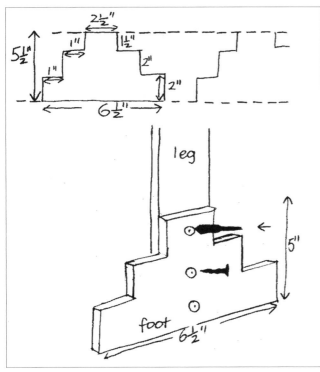

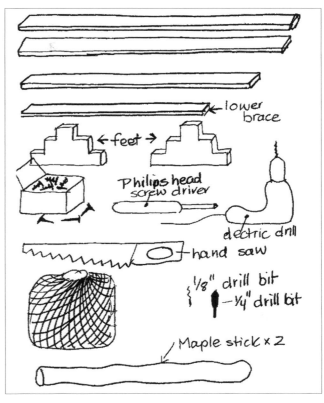

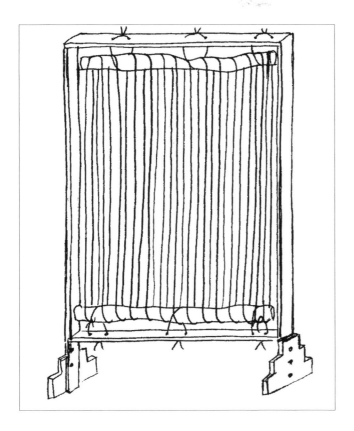

STEP ONE: Cut out all the pieces

- 2 pieces for the legs: 1" x 3" x 24"
- 1 piece for the top: 1" x 3" x 18"
- 1 piece for the brace support: 1" x 3" x 16½"
- 2 pieces for the feet: 1" x 5" x 6½" wide, pine

You can cut different-shaped feet, as long as they give enough support so the loom stands easily upright without falling over. Cut the feet on the band saw. Cut the other pieces by hand.

STEP TWO: Attach feet

Predrill holes into the feet in the three places as shown with a ¼" drill bit. Attach the two feet to the legs with 1" sheetrock screws. Make sure feet are at a right angle to the legs so the legs stand up straight.

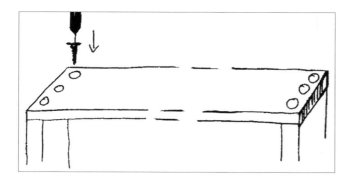

STEP THREE: Attach top

Predrill holes into the top piece with ¼" drill bit in the three places on either end as shown. Attach the top to the two legs with 1" sheetrock screws. Make sure edges are flush.

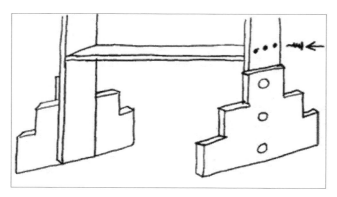

STEP FOUR: Attach brace

Predrill holes into legs from the outside just above the feet. Attach the brace with screws, making sure brace is horizontal.

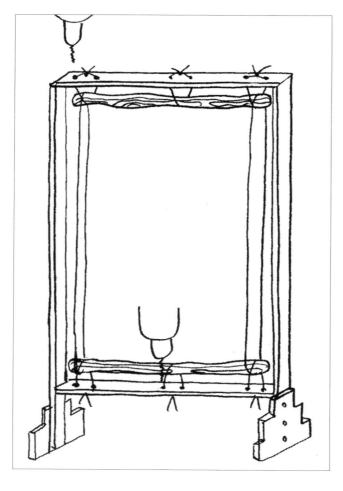

STEP FIVE:

Predrill holes into top piece and brace below in places as shown with 1/8" drill bit. Attach one of the maple sticks under the top with the yarn. It should hang down so that there is about a ¾" space between the stick and the top piece. Hang the other stick from the top stick, leaving ¾" space between the stick and the bottom brace. Secure the lower stick by taking yarn and tying the stick to the brace underneath.

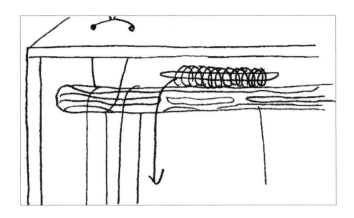

STEP SIX: Begin the warp

Wrap a small, narrow stick 5" long with yarn. The stick must be thin enough to pass through the spaces left between the cross sticks and frame. Begin by attaching the yarn to the base stick and bringing the yarn up and over the top stick, from the back to the front. Bring the yarn down over the bottom stick, from the front to the back. Continue on to the end, holding the tension as tight as possible. When the warp is completed, fasten it securely at the end to the bottom stick.

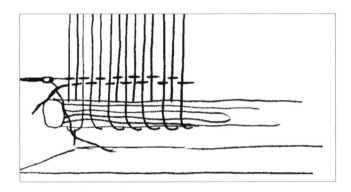

STEP SEVEN:

Begin the weaving using a needle with a large enough eye for the yarn to go through, and as long a thread as possible. Leave a 4" end hanging out on the edge.

Go in and out consistently, pushing the strings of the warp alternately forward and backward to 'establish the weave.' This should tighten up the warp. Weaving back, bring the needle and yarn through the strings opposite of what you did on the previous row.

Leave 3" at the top. Leave all weft yarn endings hanging out on the sides.

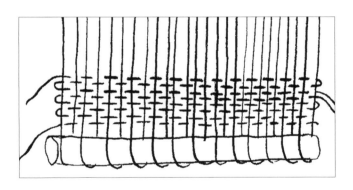

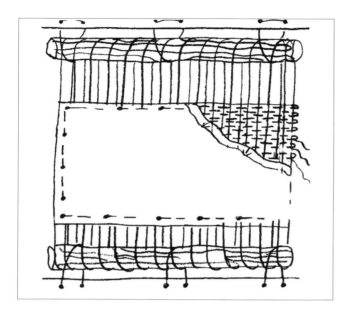

STEP EIGHT: Finishing

To make the weaving into a wall hanging, pin a piece of felt, turning over a ½" edge, on the back of the weaving, tucking in all the 4" weft ends. Sew it onto the weaving along the edge.

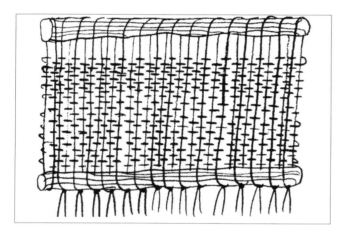

Turn weaving upside down. Cut it loose from frame. Cut the strings along the bottom and tie two together at a time, one from the front and one from the back in pairs, tight against the stick all the way along.

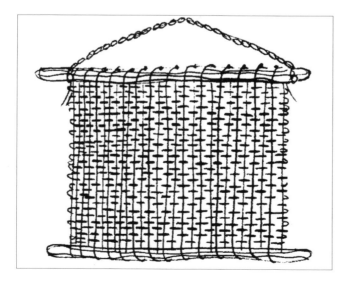

Turn hanging right way up, letting tied strings hang over the back. Attach a crocheted or finger-knitted yarn hanger at both ends of top stick—and it's ready for hanging.

Grade Four Dioramas

Materials needed:
Display boards, standard size 36" x 48", scissors, metal yardstick, exacto knife, cutting board, duct tape

Note: When scoring with exacto knife, cut only about half-way through cardboard, then bend along score and finish the cut.

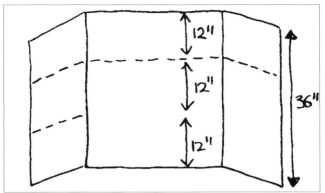

STEP ONE: Divide one board up into three sections and cut. Each section becomes one diorama with a base attached.

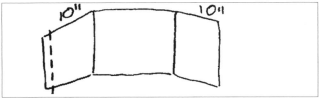

STEP TWO: Take a section and cut off one 12" panel.

STEP THREE: Score with the knife lightly the long middle panel to make a 14" wide back. Bend new right panel forward.

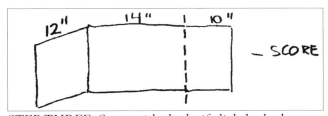

STEP FOUR: Cut the left panel to 10" wide to match the right panel at the other side.

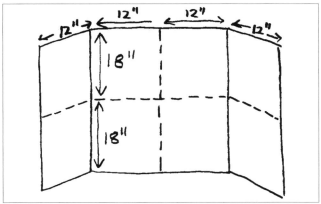

STEP FIVE: Divide another board up into eight sections for the bases and cut as shown.

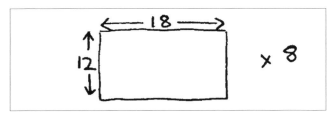

STEP SIX: Trim off a slanted edge from each base as shown. Back should now be 14" front should remain at 18".

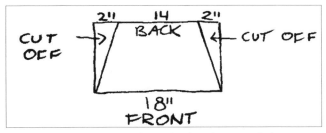

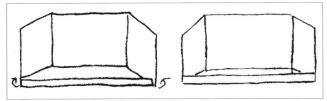

STEP SEVEN: Score underside of base at front edge to form lip. Attach and cover edge with duct tape. Decorate outside and inside panels with paintings or drawings.

RESOURCES

A.C. Harwood, *The Recovery of Man in Childhood*, The Myrin Institute, Great Barrington, MA, Second Edition, 2001. (general source on Waldorf education and child development)

Arthur M. Pittis, *Pedagogical Theatre*, AWSNA Publications, Fair Oaks, CA, 1996. (a source for how to put on plays and a variety of examples)

Arthur Auer, *Learning about the World through Modeling*, AWSNA Publications, Fair Oaks, CA, 2001.

Dick Bruin and Atti Lichthart, *Painting in Waldorf Education*, AWSNA Publications, Fair Oaks, CA, Second edition (revised), 2000.

Frank R. Wilson, *The Hand*, Pantheon Books, New York, 1998. (the critical importance of hands-on education for building the brain and real intelligence)

Herman von Baravalle, *Perspective Drawing*, Waldorf School Monographs, Englewood, NJ. (a gem of a little book on how to bring progressively more complex lessons)

Harry Kretz, *Solid Geometry for the Eighth Grade*, AWSNA Publications, Fair Oaks, CA. (for Platonic solids)

Ryukuy Saito, *Japanese Ink Painting Lessons in Suiboku Technique*, Charles E. Tuttle Company, Rutland, VT, and Tokyo, 1959.

Dennis Klocek, *Drawing from the Book of Nature*, Rudolf Steiner Press, CA. (for shaded drawing technique with a 'breathing tone')

Peter Rubino, *The Portrait in Clay*, Watson-Guptill Publications, New York, 1997.

Michael Martin and Martyn Rawson, *Educating through Arts and Crafts*, Steiner Schools Fellowship, Sussex, UK, 1999. (for modeling and woodworking ideas and lots more)

David Mitchell and Patricia Livingston, *Will-Developed Intelligence: Handwork & Practical Arts in the Waldorf School*, AWSNA Publications, Fair Oaks, CA, 1999. (for handwork and woodwork project ideas)

Elizabeth Auer, *Learning about the World through Drawing*, self-publication, 2007. (for drawing through the grades)

Edred Thorsson, *Futhark: A Handbook of Rune Magic*, Weiser Books, Boston, MA/York Beach, ME, 1984.

BIBLIOGRAPHY

Gilbert Childs. *Rudolf Steiner. Education in Theory and Practice*, UK: Floris Books, 1991.

Frans Carlgren. *Education through Freedom*, East Grinstead, UK: Lanthorn Press, 1972.

Herbert Read. *Education through Art*, New York: Pantheon Books, 1956.

CD AVAILABLE

A series of over 200 photographs (grades 1–8) covering many of the projects described in this book — for reference or inspiration or both. Arranged by grade. Available for purchase from the author:

Elizabeth Auer
RD1 Box 265 Old Temple Road
Lyndeborough, NH 03802
e-mail: elizabethauer@tds.net

$5.00 plus $2.99 shipping (by check payable to Elizabeth Auer)

Made in the USA
Columbia, SC
01 September 2020

18409011R00052